Rambling With Gambling

RAMBLING

with

GAMBLING

John Gambling

Edited by
Robert Saffron

PRENTICE-HALL, INC.
Englewood Cliffs, N.J.

Rambling With Gambling
By John Gambling, Edited by Robert Saffron
Copyright © 1972 by John A. Gambling
All rights reserved. No part of this book may be
reproduced in any form or by any means, except
for the inclusion of brief quotations in a review,
without permission in writing from the publisher.
Printed in the United States of America
Prentice-Hall International, Inc., London
Prentice-Hall of Australia, Pty. Ltd., North Sydney
Prentice-Hall of Canada, Ltd., Toronto
Prentice-Hall of India Private Ltd., New Delhi
Prentice-Hall of Japan, Inc., Tokyo

Library of Congress Cataloging in Publication Data
Gambling, John A   1930–
    Rambling with Gambling.
    Autobiography.
    I. Title.
PN1991.4.G28A3   791.44'7 [B]   72–3732
ISBN 0–13–752899–X

Fourth Printing.........September, 1972

To my patient and tolerant family—with love

CONTENTS

1. I Throw Out My Chest and Open a Window   9
2. The Joys of the Eight-Day Week   23
3. The Face on the Subway Floor   35
4. Bloopers and Bloomers and the Cat's Meow   51
5. Gambling With Gambling   67
6. Early to Bedlam   79
7. "You Can't Use Fried Potatoes in a Poker Game"   91
8. Inside the Secaucus Grand Prix: Peaches Flambée
       Exposed   103
9. Having a Baby 1000 Ft. Over the Van Wyck
       Expressway   113
10. "If John Gambling Says It, It Must Be True"   121
11. The Dear John Letters   133
12. The Day of the Flying Blintzes   151
13. Private Lives: "I Go to Bed With Your Husband"   161
14. The Family That Skis Together Convalesces
       Together   173
15. Doing Your Own Thing   183

CHAPTER ONE

I THROW OUT MY CHEST
AND OPEN A WINDOW

> . . . I learned how to count up
> to four by hearing Gambling's
> "one, two, three, four." Later
> I heard him break in John A. on
> the air as a small boy. . . . He
> lisped, as I remember it.
>
> George S. McMillan, columnist
> Yonkers (N.Y.). *Herald-States-*
> *man,* July 19, 1966

As I remember my debut, I did not lisp. I shivered—from the cold. I was four years old and had been coaxed out of a warm bed in Teaneck, N.J., at 5 A.M. on a dark, snowbound morning before Christmas.

My father had asked, "Wouldn't it be nice if you and Mother came on the Christmas program?"

"Of course," my mother said.

I didn't know what the Christmas program was. I didn't even know what strange thing Father did "in the studio" when he left early in the morning for "New York." What was a "New York"?

I'd heard his disembodied voice floating out of our Atwater Kent. He was ordering everybody to "lie on your back and pedal that bicycle . . . one! two! three! four! . . . Open the window and throw out your chest."

Throw out your chest?

How could you do that? The rest of the body would go with you! It was a terrifying idea. I didn't go near a window for days.

Here, then, was the scene in Studio 1, WOR-Radio, twenty-fifth floor, 1440 Broadway:

It was the morning of Christmas Eve, December 24, 1934. I was in short pants and Buster Brown shoes, standing stiff-backed on a wooden chair to bring my chin up to this thing Dad called a "mike." It was a shiny round metal thing, with holes around the edge big as a quarter; somehow it smelled dangerous to me, like the kitchen stove. I wouldn't have minded a stove, because I was still cold from that auto ride, and the studio wasn't too warm, either.

So I was shivering and my mother was holding onto my belt as I swayed on the chair. Behind us was the orchestra—four men, who sounded like forty to me.

My father patted me on the shoulder as he pointed to the mike. "Well, son, what would you like to do now?"

I whispered, all too close to the mike, "Go to the bathroom."

The musicians doubled over, as if in pain. One of them dropped his horn.

"Oh, ho!" my father said quickly, "you want to do that song you've been practicing all week. . . . 'The Friendly Beasts.'"

Beasts? I didn't know any beasts. I didn't remember any song.

The orchestra began playing, and I stared around in panic. I would've even thrown my chest out the window, if there had been a window. Dad briskly nodded encouragement. Mother whispered . . . " 'I,' said the sheep . . ." And the song flooded back in a rush! I murmured:

> "I," said the sheep with curly horn,
> "Gave him my wool for his blanket warm;
> He wore my coat on Christmas morn.
> "I," said the sheep with curly horn.

(Louder now. I was *singing*.)

> "I," said the cow, all white and red,
> "I gave him my manger for his bed;
> I gave him my hay to pillow his head.
> "I," said the cow, all white and red . . .

(I threw out my chest, soaring with confidence.)

Thus, every beast by some good spell
In the stable dark was able to tell
Of the gift he gave . . .

And that's how I broke into radio. In a cold sweat.

*

I progressed to "Away in a Manger" next year. At Mother's
suggestion I took piano lessons, and soon Dad suggested I play
something on the show. I don't remember what I played. I'm
sure what it was, was pretty bad. But—surprise!—my father
came home and explained how I'd helped a piano company in
New Jersey sell a piano, and they wanted me to have a present
—$5 cash. I'd done my first commercial.

I became a feature on following Christmas shows. I shared
billing with my mother, who read an original poem every year.

I reached dizzying heights with a recitation of Clement
Moore's " 'Twas the Night Before Christmas." My father had
said, "It would be nice if you went on the Christmas show with
a recitation."

I worked diligently to achieve the correct inflections and
tones. I soon realized this classic was not as well written as it
could have been. For reciting out loud, anyhow. Many of the
lines did not roll trippingly off the tongue—they just tripped:

. . . The moon on the breast of the new fallen snow
Gave a lustre of mid-day to objects below,
When what to my wondering eyes did appear
But a miniature sleigh and eight tiny reindeer;
With a little old driver so lively and quick . . .

I tried a few changes to smooth out the phrasing, but my
father wouldn't hear of it. (He's English, and they fight to the
last man to uphold the purity of the Queen's language. Years
later, I found myself insisting on reading that cigarette commercial "tastes good *as* a cigarette should." Good grammar *is* good
taste.)

Well, I worked an entire week to straighten out those damn

reindeer. Dad coached me to chuckle when I came to St. Nick's "little round belly." On the air, with some tinkling celeste music from the orchestra, the poem became my *pièce de résistance*. Thirty-five years later, our son, John, took over that same sleigh on *my* show, the second generation of Wrestling With Reindeer.

Our children, however, were rather reluctant Rudolphs. They didn't enjoy Christmas Eve in the studio as much as I had. John and Ann made their debuts at three and a half or so, singing in unison: "We wish everybody a very merry Christmas." I had to drive to the studio early, so Sally chauffeured the children into New York later.

> SALLY: Oh, the kids just didn't want to get up. It was always either snowing or raining, one would be in tears, or the other would have a sore throat or earache—or both —and they'd mumble and grumble all the way in from Long Island. I'd say, "But Daddy and Grandpa are really looking forward to us coming to the studio." And John would groan, "Why?"

Later, our youngest, Sarah, made it a trio. Her recurring critique didn't quite catch the joyous holiday spirit: *"This is dumb."* Finally, about six years ago, we let the entire Young People's Holiday Recital and Grumble fade quietly away.

*

> Amply confused at the start,
> We felt we could tell them apart.
> Daddy, John A., would be first logically,
> Followed along by a son, John B.
> But realization that son was John A.
> Filled us with sharp dismay.
> For explanation on our knees we beg:
> Which came first, the chicken or the egg?
>
> Lois and Donald Utz
> Little Falls, N.J.

It's quite simple. B came before A in our family alphabet. My father is B. because his middle name is Bradley. I am A. for Alfred McCann, Sr., a very close friend of Dad's in the early days at WOR and father of the Al McCann now on the station.

I was born in 1930 in Teaneck, N.J., a small suburban community. Two things distinguished our house from the others on the block: the tallest radio antenna and the longest automobile.

I saw Dad go off to work only once a year—when I rode with him to the Christmas show. He drove a wondrous blue Chrysler phaeton, with huge wire wheels, four doors, and, atop the rear of the front seat—a second windshield. Beautiful. The upholstery was pigskin, which left wrinkles on my back skin, and the body was eggshell blue. Convertibles were one of my father's few concessions to American flamboyance; he owned a succession of them, down to the beginning of World War II. The Chrysler floated majestically across the Hudson on the Dyckman Street ferry every morning until the George Washington Bridge opened in 1931.

The inauguration of the bridge was one of our earliest father-and-son efforts. I was the first child to cross it—my mother wheeled me in a pram—and Dad broadcast the ceremonies from the top of one of the towers. Today, Fearless Fred Feldman and George Meade sit up in helicopter 710, reporting the traffic over "the old G.W." I feel that bridge is practically in the family.

At the close of 1934, we moved to an apartment on Riverside Drive at 119th Street, overlooking the Hudson and Riverside Church. Ours was the last house on the Drive before the church, looking north, and the windiest, freezingest spot in town to a small boy walking to school. I have a vivid recollection of the clang-clang of galvanized iron garbage-pail lids, sent flying by that wind. Open land stretched up past Grant's Tomb, and on a clear day you could see all the way to Yonkers.

About this time, Dad taught me gentlemanly games—chess and cribbage. He played to win; no nonsense about losing occasionally to encourage the child. Sometimes we went bowling. He didn't bowl well and I really don't think he enjoyed it much; he wanted to provide a partner for me. Thirty years ago, there were two kinds of people—adults and children. I stayed on my side of the generation gap and he stayed on his. We got along beautifully.

I was winging it very much on my own by the age of ten or eleven; Manhattan Island was my playground, open and friendly and full of wonder. On Riverside Drive I could hear the trolley bells all the way over on Broadway. I remember the horse-drawn milk wagons early in the morning, with their muffled clip-clop of rubber-shod hooves. And the organ grinder who came around every summer, complete with a monkey in a funny suit. He would crank away under our windows on 119th Street, and my mother would give me pennies (they couldn't have been nickels) to toss down.

My turf was the block in front of our building, where I developed into a two-manhole stickball hitter. From Riverside Drive, I'd amble over to Horace Mann Elementary School, at that time on 120th Street and Broadway, all by myself. I gleefully toured up and down Fifth Avenue and the Drive in the doubledecker buses, with the little old ladies in funny hats. They waved at me and I waved at them. The buses had an open top, and a conductor took your dime in a little hand machine that made a satisfying ring when you popped your money in the slot. And in summer I looked over Broadway's wonders from the open trolleys, munching a nickel chocolate fudge cone.

From our apartment windows, you could see the 125th Street ferry plodding back and forth to New Jersey. And in the winter it was fun to try to guess which route the ferry captain would take to miss the ice floes.

I played in Riverside Park at night. Sure, there were some "tough" kids around, but we knew who they were; we avoided them if we wanted to and tried to show them that we were pretty tough, too. But nobody thought of carrying a knife, or stealing anything bigger than an apple from the fruit stand.

Now, memory is a funny thing. We tend to remember what we like to remember, and the mind blots out the unpleasant recollections. But even allowing for this rose-colored-glass effect, I still find it disheartening that all these good things, only thirty years ago, are gone.

Summers we migrated to the South Shore of Long Island. My father bought his first boat in 1937. It was named *John B.* (no false modesty here), a secondhand 34-foot Elco with a horizontal steering wheel like a Mack truck's. On our maiden voyage in the Great South Bay, we chugged along toward one of the causeway bridges Robert Moses had flung up. I was all of seven, I guess, but I sized up our mast and informed Dad, who was steering, "We're not going to make it under that bridge."

"Oh, of course we will, son."

Snap, crackle, and pop. It was that awful moment that comes to every boy, when he realizes his father can be wrong.

To give the *John B.* more scope, Dad rented summer places in Wantagh, Amityville, and Massapequa. Then my parents bought a house on the bay in Massapequa. We were always water-oriented; on my fifteenth birthday I got my first sailboat—a 16-foot Comet class sloop.

New worlds opened up. There was very little of that bay, from Seaford east to Bayshore, that I didn't explore. And in the process I sighted a few of the local girls.

There was wide-open space and lots of open water then. Massapequa was still a farm community with a scattering of summer visitors. And steam engines ran on the same Babylon branch line of the Long Island that I announce today is "running late." It was all a long way from our Riverside Drive apartment, and that was the secret of its appeal for me.

Until the wondrous day I received an auto driver's license, that 16-foot Comet was my magic carpet. It leaked badly, from the moment we bought it to the day we sold it; the sails never really set right, and most of the boys I knew had bigger and faster boats. But it was my first boat, all mine, and I loved her.

I tore myself away for two months at a boys' summer camp in New Hampshire, operated by "Moose" Miller, the baseball coach at Horace Mann. I was not the world's most enthusiastic camper; two vivid memories of those days have stayed with me. One: I got scared out of my city-boy aplomb by a counselor telling ghost stories during a thunderstorm in an old house at the top of some dumb mountain we hiked up. Two: At the end of one canoe trip, we slept in cow flop.

Back to our apartment on Riverside Drive: Everybody on the

block was building model airplanes or radio sets. Well, I glued up some balsa struts and Japanese rice paper and called it a Fokker biplane, but it never got off the grass in Riverside Park. Even though Dad helped at the launching.

I never actually built a radio. But I did put together my own broadcasting system of sorts—at thirteen. The guys at school collected records (78 rpm's in those days): Benny Goodman, Bob Crosby's Bobcats, Harry James, Tommy Dorsey, Spike Jones. I was (and still am) a great Sinatra fan. While his devotees screamed and fainted at his Paramount theater performances, I stayed home and catalogued his records. The filing consumed more time than the listening. I laboriously typed out 3 by 5 cards, listing the song title, the orchestra's name, the musicians, arranger, date. I even timed the records.

Then I had a second thought: Why not put all this effort to good use? I hooked up the record player in my bedroom to my little Philco table radio, bought a cheap carbon microphone that I could hold in front of the record-player's speaker—and wired the whole mess into the Stromberg-Carlson in the living room. I was instant Martin Block.

One problem. Nobody heard me, except myself. And my suffering mother, a captive audience in the living room. Dad was not too enthusiastic about my programming. He preferred music that made you want to exercise: Lehar waltzes, polkas from *The Bartered Bride*, Broadway show tunes. The kind played by string quartets in hotel dining rooms. I used to call it behind-the-palms music. I'm not too sure he approves of the music I play on the show today, so times haven't really changed.

I'm sure the Freudians would label the homemade disc-jockeying a subconscious imitation of my father's show, and my music a rejection of his values—a classic love-hate relationship. The truth is, I *liked* both my mother and my father; it wasn't until I reached Psych I in high school that I learned, to my astonishment, I *wasn't supposed to.*

Along about Pearl Harbor, I started at the Horace Mann School for Boys in Riverdale. I made the football varsity for two years and was a fair halfback for my weight: 135 pounds all wet with shoulder pads. In addition, I was manager of the varsity basketball team, co-chairman of the dance committee, managing editor of the school paper, writer for the yearbook, and somehow I found time to talk to girls. Some other kind of Jack Armstrong.

I found study fairly easy and did most of it with one hand above my head. I hooked my left arm through a subway strap and, hanging there for forty screeching, swaying minutes twice a day from 116th Street to Riverdale, I could compose with my right hand a devastating review of *Silas Marner*. Didn't everybody read *Silas Marner?*

The subway was much more fun than school. We'd snatch a guy's briefcase and throw it on the station platform, just as the car doors closed. He'd have to scramble for the next train back to that stop. Surprise!—the briefcase would still be there. I'm afraid the subways have lost that innocence.

I was always rigging up gadgets with dry cells and timers. Today the kids attach them to pipe bombs. I used to wire the dry cells to a doorbell, a pushbutton, and an old, black upright telephone—all collected for $1.25 downtown on Radio Row on Cortlandt St. The stuff was shoved into my briefcase, with the button hidden outside.

In a quiet moment, while the train was in a station, I'd press the button. The bell woke up the straphangers. I'd take out the phone, answer it casually, then hand it to the best-dressed woman in the car:

"Here, it's for you!"

It's a game for young and old. Years later, when I drove in to the studio from Manhasset each day, I had a phone installed in the car. Very useful. For $30 a month, plus the cost of the calls, I could listen to a party line, with gentlemen calling ladies who (I assumed) were not their wives.

Sometimes my secretary, Evelyn Volpe, would call me. One time I was pulling into the Queens Midtown Tunnel toll booth. *Rinngg!* That car phone always startled me.

As the man in the toll booth stuck his head out to collect my quarter, I handed the phone to him: "Here, it's for you." I couldn't tell whether he thought I was crazy or he was. He waved me on in a frenzy—forgetting the 25¢.

Horace Mann, as I recall it, was more fun and games than study. Staggering home from football practice one evening, we spotted the French instructor's car parked outside the library. It was one of the earliest mini-cars, the Austin built in America. Ten of us carried it up the steps and into the library.

Next day, the car was gone . . . the French teacher was serenely driving it around campus. We didn't dare ask how he had gotten it out—and nobody told us. We had been Captain Midnighted.

I received my Junior Operator driver's license and met Sally at about the same time. She was in high school in Glen Ridge, N.J. It was a rather complicated story, involving a girl I was dating on Long Island who knew a boy who lived next door to Sally in New Jersey, all of which resolved itself into a double-date after a football game between Horace Mann and Stony Brook on Long Island. We immediately started going steady. I was seventeen and she was sixteen.

My mother had a basic black 1939 Plymouth four-door with a stick shift on the floor. It was my first set of wheels and lasted me into college. That old Plymouth covered a lot of miles, which was about the only way we could go steady.

We were living in Amityville that summer, and Sally was with her family on the Jersey shore. I had a job at the Amityville Battery and Ignition Co. I swept up, waited on customers at the counter, and made deliveries in a half-ton Chevy pickup. It had a leak in the hood of the cab, so nicely placed that any rain dripped through to the floor, right where I kept my foot on the accelerator. When it rained, my foot was soaked . . . and it must have rained every Friday that summer. I'd race to our garage after work and pick up our Plymouth, then I'd race out to Jersey to pick up Sally. Her mother didn't know what to make of me—I was always stomping on her front doormat with one wet foot.

Somehow, all this varied experience got me into Dartmouth. On September 7, 1947, I took two giant steps. First, I registered as a pre-med student; I wanted to be a surgeon. Second, I applied for an announcer's job at the college radio station, WDBS.

When I walked into the studio, I was bowled over by a wave of resonant voices, of other would-be freshmen announcers. But I was John Gambling. I'd been on radio for years. I had it made.

I got a job—filing records. Of course, there was more to it than that: I also had to dust them.

At the end of my second semester, I flunked Chemistry II, and the Dean of Men advised me that frankly I was not surgeon's material. Suture self, I thought.

I transferred to a drama major. I designed stage sets and stitched costumes for *The Country Wife*. My panniers and jabots were quite fetching.

I also became an actor on the legitimate stage. In one play. With one line. And I had to ad-lib, at that. The play, *The Middle Ground*, by a fellow student, Frank Gilroy, dramatized the fissures of the forties with sharp-edged slices of life. Frank had grown up like me on the subways of New York, so the story was set in the West 145th Street IRT station.

I was The Sailor who wandered into the station and *reacted* to all the philosophy of the leading characters. "Don't talk," Frank warned me. "Just show your inner feelings in your face." It's the sort of thing Gielgud and Olivier do so well. I had one piece of business—"pick up cigarette butt and light it." Frank cast me in the part because I had to be around every performance anyhow; I was stage manager.

On opening night, my reactions were, frankly, uneasy. Second night, somebody—an enemy of fine theater?—glued that cigarette butt to the floor. I dug away at it with my fingernails, mumbling, "It must've stuck in chewing gum." I realized that was rather weak, so, fumbling, I built it up with . . . "the sonovabitch!"

Frank recovered sufficiently in later years to win the Pulitzer Prize for his play *The Subject Was Roses*. I tilted my career toward radio.

Station WDBS was an extracurricular activity of the college —more exactly, an almost penniless orphan. The staff had to hustle commercials to pay for new equipment. College radio was not the prestigious "communications teaching tool" it is today; we operated it for sheer joy and our own amazement.

In my sophomore year I broadcast a morning music and news show one or two days a week. Later, I expanded my horizons, doing "color" broadcasts for home basketball and hockey games. ("Color" is the emotional background: titles at stake, the players' problems and injuries, celebrities in the stands, etc.)

My career reached its zenith in a series of thirty weekly half-hour dramatic productions. The Dartmouth library had a large collection of old radio mystery and dramatic scripts: *I Love a Mystery* (remember Jack, Doc, and Reggie?), *Inner Sanctum*, and others by Arch Obeler and Orson Welles. I was producer, casting office, sound-effects man, and typist of the mimeograph stencils. My schedule: Friday, dig through the old bones in the library to unearth the shocker of the week. Over the weekend, bang out the stencils. Monday, run them off. Tuesday, cast the show and direct a couple runthroughs. Wednesday, dress rehearsal, with properly creaking doors and bloody stabs. Thursday, the Big Broadcast. Friday, back to the library, sifting bones again.

Who listened? Well, we covered all the dorms and most of the town of Hanover, and on a clear night we were heard all the way across the Connecticut River in Norwich, Vermont. I guess our Hooper rating wasn't high, but the audience was certainly larger than the one in the Riverside Drive living room.

Another student working on the station was Buck Zuckerman, who ad-libbed a zany disc-jockey program. I cast him frequently in the mysteries because he was a fine character actor with an amazingly wide range of voices. His middle name was Henry; later, as Buck Henry, he wrote the screenplay for *The Graduate* and *Catch-22* and acted in them, too.

*

There was a great Nat Cole recording in those days—"Too Young." Remember? One of the lines ran, "They tried to tell us we're too young." Every couple, I'm sure, has a tune they call "our song." This is mine and Sally's.

When I breezed off to Dartmouth, Sally still had a year to finish at Glen Ridge High School. Our position was not desperate, though. I could run down to New Jersey for an occasional weekend, and she was permitted to visit Hanover now and then. In my soph year, Sally was accepted at Colby Junior College, a girls' school just twenty miles from Dartmouth. The future looked rosy. Or so we thought.

I never knew whether there was any collusion between her parents and mine, but I sensed that they felt our romance was just a bit too serious. Too young. So, instead of Colby College, Sally found herself enrolled in Southern Seminary and Junior College, way down near Buena Vista, Virginia. Our three-a-week phone calls made a sharp cut into our allowances.

We braved it for a year. I never got down to Buena Vista; there was nothing to do in that town, and the seminary rules on visitors were as restrictive as a nunnery's. Sally did make the long train and bus trek to Hanover as often as she could. I even managed to get myself put on probation by the dean at Dartmouth because I registered one day late for a new semester. I'd stayed over in New York just to take Sally to dinner.

By my junior year, the miles between the Blue Ridge Mountains of Virginny and the White Mountains of New Hampshire were just too many. We concocted some sort of cover story, which our parents may or may not have believed, and during a vacation break we took off for North Carolina. That was the nearest state in which we could be married in a hurry.

I was nineteen and she was eighteen. Our parents faced up to the *fait accompli* with some surprise and reasonably good will. I was able to make speedy arrangements for a married student's apartment, in barracks operated by Dartmouth, and Sally bade a dry-eyed farewell to Southern Seminary. She decided to drop out of school to become a full-time wife. Dad agreed to continue paying tuition for my senior year; I still had to work for my room and board. He firmly believed in the old English virtues: work hard, play fair, play the game, and play it square.

I'd been promoted to station manager of WDBS for my senior year, but it paid a salary of zero. I had to find a job. After three years of college, I was really prepared for only one career—

radio. But who would hire a nineteen-year-old with absolutely no professional experience? It was a crisis familiar to radio soap-opera addicts:

> ANNOUNCER: This is the story that asks the question: Can a young man from the big city find happiness while struggling to maintain himself and his new wife in simple dignity and still win a college degree in a small New England town?
> MUSIC: Crescendo of tension . . .

CHAPTER TWO

THE JOYS OF THE EIGHT-DAY WEEK

> I've been listening closely to
> your show since I was 12 years
> old, and it has given me a deep
> interest in a career in radio or
> television. I am applying to col-
> leges now, and one of them is
> Dartmouth. I would like to
> meet you at WOR in hopes of
> getting a recommendation to
> your alma mater. I know Dart-
> mouth won't get me a job like
> yours, but I am sure it can't
> hurt.
>
> John D. Sainer
> Pittsfield, Mass.

It can hurt, all right. Even before you graduate.

In June 1950, as summer vacation approached, I heard that the Granite State Network was looking for a summer-replacement announcer. I cornered one of the owners, Bill Rust, in his office in Manchester, N.H. I turned on my best prickly-pear-shaped tones, and added that I would work cheap; he was sufficiently persuaded to let me fill in at two of their stations in New Hampshire. The most important was WKBR, the key station in Manchester, population 82,732. The other was WTSV in Claremont, population 12,811.

We were to move into the Manchester apartment vacated for three weeks by a high-living bachelor announcer. I considered this a really progressive, even glamorous, step because Sally and I and baby John R. were cooped up in the ex-Navy barracks that Dartmouth rented to married students.

My shift would be 4 P.M. to midnight, leaving plenty of time for daytime recreation with my family. Plus—my voice would be heard and recognized throughout the greater Manchester metropolitan area (a potential of over 80,000 fans was big-time at last). And since I had said I'd work cheap, I got $35 a week.

When we pulled into Manchester in our Chevrolet, loaded with baby-food bottles, diapers, suntan lotion, and my throat spray, we found that the "fabulous" apartment was actually a tiny bedroom and kitchen in a peeling private house. Without private entrance. Neither Sally nor I knew a soul in Manchester, which turned out to be a rather bleak textile town. So my nine-teen-year-old wife spent every night at home, alone with the baby in a strange town. She got a lot of ironing and reading done, and she could listen to me.

I also discovered that the man for whom I was subbing dou-bled on another job I hadn't been told about. He perpetrated a noon-to-12:30 show for which he'd gone out and sold commer-cials all by himself, bypassing the station's salesmen. He'd already collected the contracts, and I had to fulfill them. For free.

It was a half-hour of solid commercials, interrupted by only one minute and forty-five seconds of music. My benefactor was very fond of Bing Crosby. One recording—only one—was played right in the middle of this morass of monotony. A Bing Crosby.

And so I began my first paid professional job with an incredi-ble technological breakthrough—I was transported back, back into the Stone Age of radio. It made a full, full day for me. But recognition?—80,000 fans? . . . Somehow, three weeks just wasn't long enough to make much of a mark in Manchester.

From there, the Gambling Road Show moved on to WTSV in Claremont for another three-week stint. Luckily, I was able to commute from our barracks apartment in Hanover. My only remaining memory of Claremont still makes me cringe: a sibilant commercial for the "Singer Sewing Center on South Center Street." I sounded like a leaky gas pipe.

Several years ago a man called to inform me that WTSV was up for sale and would I join him in buying it? I recall thinking: Had I been such a smashing success there—or was he giving me a chance to atone? I declined.

There is another town in New Hampshire, however, that is a permanent part of my professional memories: Lebanon, population 8,495. Lebanon was my Rubicon. Whatever my doubts and disappointments in radio after Lebanon, I could not turn back.

Friendly little Leb, as we called it, had first floated into my consciousness two years before, as a small New England town, about five miles from Hanover, renowned for the one liquor store in the Hanover area. State law permitted local option on alcohol sales. And Hanover chose to be dry. The weekly "Leb run" for booze is a part of every Dartmouth man's college recollections.

Early in the fall of 1950, the Granite State Network began to build a 500-watt station, WTSL. Bud Popke was made station manager. Bud had also managed the Dartmouth college radio station two years earlier and needed a morning man for WTSL. (He's still in radio, operating several stations in Michigan.) He called me:

"How would you like a part-time job as announcer in Lebanon? Write some copy . . . sell some ads. It's only 6 to 9 in the morning."

Only? I should have known by now. When a station manager says *only*—look out. Instead, I said, "Gee, great! And I work cheap."

"It's yours."

I tried not to worry that I was also going to be station manager of Dartmouth's WDBS for the coming year, and this might create some conflict of interest. It also was very much a full-time job—without pay. And I had a commitment to a third job, which was sort of full-time: graduating from Dartmouth.

Well, when you're young you don't really worry about minor details like working twenty-four hours a day, eight days a week.

When people ask me, "Exactly what kind of an operation was WTSL?" I can only say, "Thrifty." But since I worked cheap, I fit right in. While the permanent building was being erected, we worked in a 12- by 19-foot trailer parked beside the transmitter in the middle of a cornfield between Leb, Hanover, and White River Junction. Let me list the marvels crammed into that space, just a little larger than the Apollo 16 lunar craft:

At one end, two turntables, a control console, and one micro-phone, hanging from the roof. Center, three feet away, one kero-sene stove (for a *simulation* of heat, but mostly for whimsy and smoke), and, next to it, a rack for records. At the "far" end, the business office—one typewriter, one phone, and one desk. Thrift-ily designed for maximum efficiency in minimum space. When I was on the air in the morning, I was the only john around. When nature called, I answered in the cornfield.

One thing we did have was lots of cold. The bone-cracking, icicle-down-your-spine New Hampshire cold. It often went down to 10 and 15 below zero, and I wished I had a handy ice-house to warm up in. I had made my radio debut at four, shiver-ing—and here I was in radio at twenty, still shivering.

I would stumble out of bed at 5 A.M., prop my eyelids up with three cups of coffee, and speed over to the trailer to fire up the transmitter. For three hours, from 6 to 9, I was WTSL—the entire staff. Sally would be home listening—to keep me com-pany—and she always knew when I was "out in the field," be-cause I'd put an LP record on the turntable and let it play two or three numbers. Still, there was always the question of who would finish first, I or the record.

Luckily, my first class didn't begin until 9:30 A.M., so I had half an hour to hightail back to Hanover. My last class ended at 2:30, after which I'd scoot to the barracks for a quick lunch with Sally. Then I would scramble back to the trailer, to write commercial copy until about 6. Then zip home for dinner. Sally had worked out an arrangement with two of my former room-mates; they paid $10 a week and she cooked for all of us. Mostly stews and casseroles. Still, taking in dinner boarders paid for our food, and believe it or not I still like a baked tuna and noodle casserole. And our children do, too.

I finished dinner about 7:30 and buckled down to my second job—homework. Fortunately, I can concentrate almost any-where. It was probably due to those years of hanging from a subway strap and working on *Silas Marner*. I rarely found it necessary to enter the library. Maybe the passage of time has anesthetized my recollection. Maybe I didn't study at all. Some of my professors thought the same thing.

My third job—managing Dartmouth's WDBS—was squeezed in between the other two. I'd have to go back to campus several nights a week for meetings, although my WDBS broadcasting was limited. I also worked Saturday morning at WTSL (no extra pay, of course), doing a classical musical program. After a while the station acquired a wire recorder, a predecessor of today's tape recorder, and I could prerecord the show in spare minutes. The quality of reproduction was atrocious, but it gave me time to breathe.

I also sold commercials for WTSL, and when I had nothing else to do, I swept out the trailer.

Another student, Jim Rhodes, worked the mike in the afternoon while I was writing news or ad copy. Every time he went on the air, I had to stop typing so the racket wouldn't be broadcast, too. The business phone was left off the hook for fear of an unexpected ring; for an important call, I carried the phone out into the snow.

It was all very casual, but we learned fast. Often I would be pounding out commercial copy that Jim would need two minutes later. We also invented little games to try to break each other up. I wrote the reviews of local movies—based mainly on the blurbs in the newspaper ads. My review of *School for Dogs* was embellished with, "starring that pre-eminent dog of stage, screen, and radio—Jim Rhodes!" Jim, as usual, read it "cold." Then he collapsed, gurgling, as if going under water for the third time. Score one for the copywriter.

That was the year Harry Truman fired General MacArthur. Bud Popke ordered me to hustle into Lebanon for man-in-the-street reactions to this palpitating moment in history. "While you're there," he added, "try to sell some ads."

I grabbed the wire recorder and headed for Leb. After each street interview, I'd pop into the nearest store and buttonhole the owner: "Did you hear that interview I just did in front of your store? Don't you want to participate in this important day in history? And, oh yes, I mentioned your business in the interview."

Almost all of them bought a spot. They only cost $2.50. Two hours later the show went on the air—fully sponsored.

WTSL had certain occupational hazards. Because of our frequent and plentiful supply of snow, Popke had arranged with the town authorities to plow the narrow dirt road leading through the cornfield to our trailer. One morning the snow was piled up so high I just couldn't drive in. I abandoned my Chevy on the road between Hanover and White River Junction and stomped through the drifts. The show must go on—the commercials must get through! . . . They did, until about 8 A.M., when a horrible clanking and roaring filtered into the trailer. I saw a giant snowplow come shuddering up to my window and stop short. But not short enough. Tilt! The room hung there, at a 20-degree angle, then dropped back to the ground. The turntable pickup arm had skidded off the record. I grabbed the microphone to make some inane apology to my listeners.

The friendly driver waved to show he hadn't meant it personally and clanked back down our road. And for about ten seconds, I wondered if this was really what "show biz" should be like.

Another vivid memory of my last year in school was the willful frustrations of the ex-Navy barracks in which Sally and I lived. They had been erected years before at the U.S. Naval Base in Portsmouth, N.H. At the beginning of World War II, the college had them dismantled and trucked to Hanover, to provide desperately needed shelter for the Navy's "ninety-day-wonder" officer candidates. The barracks seem to have carried naval regulations with them; they had a bachelor will of their own. After the war they stubbornly resisted every effort to domesticate them for women and children. The wooden buildings, shaggy around the edges and sagging in the middle like old horses, huddled on the edges of a cliff overlooking the Connecticut River. For obvious reasons, this outpost became known as Fertile Circle.

The insides had been converted, with minimum effort, into two-room apartments: living room, bedroom, bath, and tiny kitchen. The walls were sheetrock, nailed over 2 by 4 studs; no foundation, just a wood floor covered with linoleum. The only source of heat, a kerosene stove in the middle of the living room, was square and brown and cranky. All this for $65 a month. We thought it was wonderful; it was our first home.

John slept in a crib in the bedroom, which had a lovely view of the river—when the window wasn't covered by frost. The winds howled across that river, sweeping right through our meager walls and floor. John was swaddled in those Dr. Denton flannel sleepsuits (I think they were called "bunny bags"), but he'd wake up in the middle of the night, screaming, blue with cold. It couldn't have been too unhealthy, though, because we all survived with a minimum of colds and sniffles.

Our parents were positive that the kerosene heater would blow up some night and cremate us all. When we tried to temper the chill winds with electric heaters, we ran into another dreaded crisis—the Big Blowout.

The buildings had been wired and fused for primitive illumination and cooking. No stove, no oven, just a two-burner hotplate in the kitchen. Of course, everyone started improving his lot according to his means, with toasters, revolving-spit broilers, electric irons, hairdryers, and even ovens. So, if Sally turned on the space heater while she bathed the baby, a neighbor was sure to be cooking a roast. Pow! Out went the fuse, not just for our apartment but for the entire building. No bath, no roast, no light, and some poor guy trying to study for an exam.

Someone would finally call the college custodian. If we were lucky, a man would appear an hour or so later to replace the fuse. The fusebox was locked, of course, to prevent us clever electricians from introducing high-amperage fuses, crossed wires or pennies. These would have prevented the blackouts, but probably burn down the barracks. There were times when that seemed like a pretty good idea.

But the buildings, sagging and shivering, held together despite everything. So we cheerfully invested in some paint—dark brown was the "in" color that year for living rooms. We even wallpapered the kitchen. All three square feet of it.

The uninsulated walls added unique stresses to some of the marital problems created by young children, lots of schoolwork, and no money. There was a break in the morning class schedule between 10 and 10:30. Almost every morning, at about 10:03, one of our neighbors would come charging down the hill from

campus to the barracks and race upstairs to his apartment, two
steps at a time.

At first, the Fertile Circle crowd thought he was saving
money by coming home for a morning snack of coffee and Dan-
ish. But how hungry can a fellow be to run a half-mile each
way? There was a second possibility, suggested by another of
our neighbors, a genuine cynic who advocated the empirical
method—experience over theory—to solve this question. One
day, when Roger the Runner's wife went out early to shop, we
tied a bunch of tin cans to the underside of their mattress. A
very quiet group of about ten scholars gathered in the adjacent
apartment, next to the bedroom being tested. Soon the rattle of
the cans and the outraged male screams proved that our neighbor's hypothesis was absolutely correct. Roger was trying to
keep the circle fertile.

About this time, my parents decided that John should have a
safe, proper baby carriage. A delivery truck deposited a huge
English pram outside the barracks: high wheels, spring-sus-
pended body, tilting canvas canopy. The Rolls-Royce of baby
carriages. All our neighbors came out to inspect its wonders. To
top it all, one of my father's sponsors was a furrier, and he had
insisted on creating a monogrammed mink carriage wrap. Dad
had affectionately nicknamed the baby Demijohn, to sort out
the newest John in the Gambling family. So there it was—
DEMIJOHN, right on the fur. I'm sure nothing like this ensemble has since been seen at Dartmouth.

The pram and baby were proudly resting outside, that first
afternoon, when a rainstorm blew up. I scurried out to rescue
them—only to discover I couldn't push the pram beyond the
front door. Our apartment door was at a perfect 90-degree angle
to the barracks' entrance, so the monstrous carriage couldn't
make the turn. Unless I kicked down the sheetrock wall.

Father, baby pram, and monogrammed fur were thoroughly
soaked, but I finally parked the pram in an apartment with a
wider entrance. Next day I had to buy several expensive sheets
of plywood and some 2-by-4's and hammer them together for a
lean-to at the back of the barracks. Our new Chevrolet, a wed-

ding present from Sally's parents, sat out in the snows all winter, but the pram was splendidly snug in its own garage.

That same winter, we decided it was time to have our own Christmas tree. A real live one, of course. Our friends, the Bud Popkes, volunteered to join in the search. He had an old convertible that would be suitable, top down, for transporting the trees.

We bundled John, eight months old, into the convertible and drove out to tree country. We discovered two magnificently shaped specimens in some unknowing farmer's field, hacked them down, and dragged them into the car. We jammed the trunks into the back seat; I wedged in there with them. The Popkes, Sally, and baby squeezed into the front seat.

About twenty miles from Hanover it started to snow, hard. It grew colder and John turned bluer . . . we were all but covered with snow, but we dragged those trees back to the apartment. We wedged them into homemade tree stands and up they went . . . well, almost up. The ceiling must have been all of 7 feet high . . . the tree was 12 or 14 feet. It had looked just right out in the farmer's field, but in our apartment it was a monster. I think I trimmed off enough for another Christmas and I must have spent a full week's salary on the decorations. We didn't have money left for a party, but who cared?—there was no room in the apartment for anybody except us and our one-tree forest.

We did have parties on occasion. Sally gave me a gala celebration on my twenty-first birthday. We had all our neighbors and friends in—and with my usual luck, I had a midterm exam the next day and, of course, the morning show at WTSL. (This past winter, we called John on his twenty-first birthday, in his apartment in Boston. His wife, Chris, had given him a surprise birthday party the previous night, when he was busy preparing for an exam and a morning show for the college station. Life does have a way of repeating itself, even after twenty years.)

Looking back at that winter in Hanover, it wasn't too bad, really. The living wasn't easy, and it was a bit pinched, but we made a lot of warm friendships in Fertile Circle. We still exchange Christmas cards with a half-dozen couples—now scattered all the way from New Orleans to Oregon. We formed lifelong ties, I think, because we were all in the same boat, rowing hard to get through school and make ends meet. One fine day, we'll all get together. The weather overlooking the Connecticut might have been cold, but the memories are still very warm.

I graduated in June 1951, with a B.A. in English Drama. Everybody seemed a bit surprised that I had made it—Sally, my parents, and certainly the dean. As soon as I was handed my diploma, I was out of work again. I couldn't afford to stay at WTSL part-time at $35 a week. So, once more into the breach.

I auditioned for an announcing job at WHLI, one of the oldest and, I believe, best stations on Long Island, in Hempstead. I flunked. In 1970, its owner, Paul Godofsky, took $2 from me in a golf match. I took the occasion to inquire why he hadn't hired me.

"We were looking for a solid voice that would blend in with any format," he said. "You're too much of a personality. I wouldn't have hired Arthur Godfrey."

Of course, Arthur Godfrey didn't need the job.

WNEW turned me down, and so did several other stations. One thought I needed "more seasoning." Another suggested I might be happier in television. It was a time for soul-searching. My father offered me $75 a week to work for him as production assistant on *Rambling With Gambling*.

I did not have any hangup about nepotism, or being dominated by Dad. The thought of receiving $75 a week—every week!—was comforting to a young father who had just signed a lease for a house in Levittown. It was a foot in the front door; if I really had any ability in broadcasting, the chance I wanted would come.

My father had a four-piece orchestra on the program with him in 1951; he was just beginning to supplement this live music with LP records. I selected the records (within the limits of his style of music), helped around the office, answered mail, and generally made myself useful. After the frenetic round-the-clock years in Hanover, it was a breeze.

At the beginning: My father was seventeen when this formal portrait was taken—the year was 1914, World War I was just beginning, and young John B. Gambling had signed on as wireless operator in His Majesty's Navy.

This photo was taken in 1923, on the roof at Bamberger's Department Store in Newark, New Jersey, where WOR had its beginnings. With rather primitive "portable" equipment, my father, with Chief Engineer Jack Poppele, seems to be pointing off into the future of radio.

I appear on the scene on Easter Sunday 1931. My father saved those plus-fours and that peaked cap for special occasions and for driving the eggshell blue Chrysler Phaeton. This was in Teaneck, New Jersey, where we lived until 1934.

Dad, with vest, striped tie, and pin-striped suit; this was an informal daytime broadcasting moment in the early thirties. Announcers who worked at night wore tuxedoes.

Family cruising, 1934 style. Yes, that's me under the crazy hat. Note the midi skirt on my mother. This was a summer trip to Europe.

6.45—FIRST GROUP

7.15—SECOND G

1. Chest and Lung Development

Fold arms across chest, exhaling completely. Take slow, deep breath, unfolding arms and extending to horizontal position. Exhale, bringing arms to starting position.

2. Waist Line, Back Muscles and Spine

Take erect position, feet apart, arms extended horizontally. Bend forward, twisting at waist and touching outside of left foot with right hand. Return to upright position, then bend and touch outside of right foot with left hand.

3. Abdominal Twisting and Spinal Stimulation

Erect position, feet well apart, arms extended horizontally. Keep eyes front. Twist at waist line as far as possible, arms remaining rigid. Alternately twist right and left.

1. Lung and Chest Developer

Stand erect, arms at sides. Take slow, deep breath, raising arms to position over head with palms out. Exhale slowly, returning to starting position.

2. Waistline, Back Muscle Spine

Stand with feet well apart, extended over head, palms Twist at waistline, bending t touching both hands to floo yond left foot. Return to u position and repeat bendi right.

4 and 5. Leg and Hip Reducer

Lie flat on back, hands at sides, feet apart. Raise right leg to upright position. Lower to floor outside left heel. Back to upright position and return to starting position. Repeat with left leg.

6 and 7. Abdominal and Intestinal Stimulation

Lie flat on back, placing right forearm under head. Draw up left knee to chest, trying to touch right hand with left knee. Return to flat position. Repeat exercise No. 6 with left arm and right knee.

8. Leg and Hip Exercise

Take upright position. Place hands on hips. Squat, placing right hand on floor, and thrust left leg out to side. Return to upright position.

5. Waist and Back Stimulation

Stand erect, clasping hands behind head. Bend trunk forward as far as possible, then back, keeping hands behind head as you go down and up.

6. Abdominal Exercis

Lie flat on floor, hands c chest, raising arms t movement when riding a b until count is completed.

9. Repeat exercise No. 8, extending right leg and left hand.

10 and 11. Abdominal Kneading

Take upright position. Raise right knee. Clasp hands around right knee, pulling it forcibly against abdomen. Return to upright position. Repeat exercise No. 10 with left knee.

12. Thigh Exercise

Assume upright position, hands on hips. Squat, trying to sit on heels. Return to starting position.

9. Abdomen and Back Exercise

Lie flat on floor face downward, arms folded across chest, legs extended. Raise both legs up as far as possible, spreading them while raising. Return to original position.

10. For Abdomen, Back Hips

Kneel on floor with hips res heels. Fold arms across Bend forward, touching t to floor. Return to origina ing position.

13. The Workout

Down on all fours, legs extended to rear. Jump, bringing both knees up together under chest. Return to extended position.

14. The Runner

Down on all fours, legs extended. Jump, bringing knees up alternately, first left then right.

15. Perspiration Inducer

Down on all fours, legs extended. Jump, placing feet well apart, then back to starting position.

13. Hip Reducer

Stand erect, hands on hips. Raise knees alternately in running fashion as high as possible.

14. Running Exerci

Stand erect, hands on hips placing left foot forward a foot rear. Jump, alterna position of the feet.

CISE CHART:
To help you each morning
When you tune in on WOR

7.45—THIRD GROUP

and 4. Abdominal and Spinal Stimulation
and erect, arms at sides. Charge rward with right foot, flinging th arms back over head. Re- rn to starting position.
Repeat exercise No. 3, charging th left foot.

7 and 8. Hip Exercises
e on right side, arms folded across est. Swing legs alternately back- rd and forward.
Lie on left side and repeat exer- e No. 7.

11 and 12. Leg Developer
and erect, hands on hips. Squat, ending left leg to front. Touch nds to floor at side.
Repeat exercise No 11 but ex- d right leg.

15. Perspiration Inducer
nd erect, hands on hips, feet ether. Jump, spreading feet art, then jump back to original ition.

1. Lung Developer
Stand erect, arms at sides. Bend trunk forward, extending hands to floor, keeping knees rigid. Return to upright position and take slow, deep breath, meanwhile turning palms out at sides.

2. For Waist Line
Stand erect with feet well apart, arms extended to sides with palms down. Bend trunk alternately right to left, keeping arms rigid.

3 and 4. For Spine, Neck and Intestines
Assume upright position. Clasp hands behind head. Raise right knee up to chest and pull head down at same time, touching chin to knee.
4. Repeat exercise No. 3 but raise left knee.

5. For Lower Abdomen
Lie flat on floor with hands clasped under head. Raise both legs to vertical position and lower without touching heels to floor.

6. For Upper Abdomen
Lie on floor with arms extended be- yond head. Rise to sitting posi- tion, touching hands to toes and then back to original position.

7. Abdomen and Chest Strengthener
Lie flat, arms extended beyond head. Raise right leg and left arm to vertical position. Alternate with left leg and right arm.

8. For Abdomen
Lie flat. Bring arms and legs to vertical position. Cross arms and legs simultaneously, starting with right arm over left leg and left leg over right leg.

9 and 10. For Hips
Stand erect, hands on hips. Circle the right leg to front and away from body.
10. Repeat exercise No. 9 circling left leg.

11 and 12. For Abdomen and Spine
Stand erect, feet well apart, left hand on hip, right arm over head. Bend to right and touch floor on the outside of right foot with right hand. Resume original position.
12. Repeat exercise No. 11 but place right hand on hip, extend left arm over head and bend to left, touching outside of left foot.

13. Leg Exercise
Stand erect, with hands on hips. Take deep knee bend and thrust arms forward. Return to upright position with hands on hips.

14. For Abdomen and Back
Sit on floor with arms between knees and hands clasping toes. Roll back, bringing feet over head and, if possible, touch floor. Then back to sitting position. Keep grip on toes while rolling.

15. Abdominal Exercise
Lie flat. Clasp hands under head. Raise legs off floor about six inches. Then spread them apart and bring together again without touching heels to floor.

4921   Printed in U. S. A.   © 1926 *Postum Cereal Company, Inc.*

This exercise chart, for what was then called "Gam- bling's Musical Clock" or "Gambling's Gym Class," was one of radio's early mail order giveaways. Listen- ers opened their charts each morning and did the exercises along with John B. and the World's Greatest Little Orchestra.

The World's Greatest Little Orchestra in the early forties. From left to right, the Maestro, Vincent Sorey. At piano, Michael Rosco, otherwise known as Rudolph. Just in front of the canary cages is Pietro Frosini, the beloved Froz, of the vaudeville one-liners. Next, Louis Biamonte, flutist, clarinetist, saxophonist, and straight man. My father at the stand-up microphone on the right. In the control room are engineers John Cook and Jack Byrne. Johnny retired just a year or so ago after thirty-five years of "Rambling With Gambling." The last gentleman in the picture, unidentified, was in charge of making the canaries sing.

I was not going to a costume party. This was the way Boy Scouts dressed in the old days. I must be about thirteen or fourteen here, and attending Horace Mann School for Boys.

The year was 1947, and it was my first weekend home from Hanover to visit Sally. Note the bobby sox on Sally and the recent vintage World War II flight jacket that I was sporting.

My father celebrated his twenty-fifth anniversary on the air in 1950. The gentleman in the middle is my grandfather, who came over from England to attend the celebration at the Longacre Theatre in New York. How about that waxed mustache?

This was my big theatrical moment at Dartmouth: Frank Gilroy's play *The Middle World*. Far to the right, the guy in the sailor suit is me. Seated at the bottom of the steps just to my left is Buck Henry Zuckerman. Recent moviegoers who saw *The Graduate* or *Catch-22* saw films in which Buck worked as writer and actor. He is now Buck Henry.

I think this is one of my favorite pictures. It was the day I graduated from Dartmouth College, June 1951. Young John was just over a year old, and Sally was anticipating the midi skirt style of the seventies. The picture was taken in the scenic outback behind our barracks apartment.

The Gambling clan gathering at Christmas to raise their voices with the Salvation Army Cadet Choir. Ann and young John seem to have lost the melody somewhere, but our poodle, Demitasse, was intrigued with the whole affair. Merry Christmas, 1954.

WOR re-designed one of its studios for the new high-fidelity *Music From Studio X* program. Even the door was adorned for the premier broadcast. I spent many long, late hours in that studio.

March 8, 1955. Inside Madison Square Garden at 8 A.M.; the house was packed, and this wonderful morning had to be the highlight of my father's career. We estimated that 27,000 people watched all or part of the broadcast in the old Garden.

Ann was not quite three on March 8, 1955, but in her starched party dress, running around center stage in Madison Square Garden, she stole the show. Here she looks up at grandfather John B. as if to say, "Gee, this is fun!"

Again, three generations of John Gamblings. This picture was taken around the time of the Madison Square
Garden celebration in 1955.

A quiet moment at home with Sarah Jane.

From the expressions on Sarah Jane's and Ann's faces, perhaps you can understand why we decided to give up the Christmas morning family broadcast. This was taken in 1965. Sarah Jane, on the left, was five years old, her sister was twelve.

Sally and I have enjoyed our home on Manhasset Bay
in Plandome, Long Island, for some twelve years now.
Since this picture was taken, the willow tree has suc-
cumbed to a winter storm and both Sally and I have
managed to shed a few pounds.

This is the good ship *JAG*, a 37-foot Egg Harbor cabin cruiser, on which all the Gamblings spent many happy days.

The most recent group picture of the morning crew. Seated from left to right: Jack Allen, Bill McEvilly, Peter Roberts, and Fred Feldman. Standing, again left to right: Bob Harris, Don Criqui, Harry Hennessy, me, George Meade, and Henry Gladstone. Any similarity between this picture and the FBI's "10-Most-Wanted" list is purely coincidental.

Helicopter 710, chief pilot "Fearless Fred" Feldman, and his occasional passenger and navigator. Fred has logged more than ten years and many thousands of hours watching New York traffic.

The orchestra played what had originally been the setting-up-exercise segment of the show. The exercises had been abandoned years ago, but they were still billed as The World's Greatest Little Orchestra. All excellent musicians. But after years of on-air banter with my father, they had turned into Personalities. Everybody got into the act, each with a nickname, the origins of which had been forgotten in the static of the thirties.

The maestro, Vincent Sorey, somewhat unkempt at 6 in the morning, led with his violin. Even though he seemed to be afflicted with chronic somnambulism. To my father, he was always Vincent. The pianist, Michael Rosco, was tall and vaguely suave, so Dad had named him Rudolph. Louis Biamonte (Rastus) played two saxophones, the flute, clarinet, and, when pressed, the ocarina ("sweet potato"). He was short and chubby and the straight man; mostly, he kept quiet and played his instruments.

Pietra Frosini (Froz) was the self-proclaimed top banana. A former headline accordionist in vaudeville, he'd composed several "standard" accordion pieces. He was now in his seventies, skinny and small, and his eyesight was somewhat hazy. His students took turns carrying his accordion to the studio, and sometimes they seemed to carry Froz. Still, he was always "on," popping one-line jokes with the firm conviction that what had wowed 'em in vaudeville for a hundred years would murder 'em in radio, too. Sample Frosini swifties:

FROZ: "I got a splinter in my finger last night."

FATHER: "Working around the house?"

FROZ: "Yeh, my girl's house. She has a wooden leg."

Jokes like that killed vaudeville, and could have done the same for radio.

For several years, Dad broadcast the show in the summertime from the den in his country home in Old Field, L.I. The orchestra remained in the studio at 1440 Broadway; each man wore earphones so he could hear Dad. I was also in the studio, co-ordinating the confusion. I don't think Vincent ever understood the technical setup. When my father asked him a question from Old Field, Vincent would pull off his earphones and talk into them instead of the mike. It was wild.

This was my apprenticeship in New York radio. In July 1951, I advanced a notch, substituting for my father when he went on vacation. WOR was dubious about me. And I received some letters grumbling, "You may have the same name, but you'll never be as good as your father." Nevertheless, most of our audience was still listening when Dad came back.

Next year he was offered the chance to buy WGBB, a small station in Freeport, L.I. He was beginning to look ahead to retirement; this would be a convenient way to keep his hand in the business while I operated the station full-time as a family enterprise. It meant I would have to give up the dream of making the grade in New York, the top of the mountain in American broadcasting.

My father had always let me make my own decisions—good and bad—so the choice was up to me. Sally and I discussed it over the coffee cups and far into the night. We both came to the same conclusion: running a radio station on Long Island was not what I really wanted. I wanted to stay at WOR. I felt I could establish myself on my own. Or even replace Dad when he retired. Only one year out of college and I was ready to take over the world.

My father was noncommittal about my dreams. "Do what you want. I won't try to influence you. We'll just have to wait and see."

I was really reaching for the stars. After twenty-eight years on the air, Dad was Number One in New York radio. He brought in $2 million in advertising billing, an incredible 28 percent of WOR's total income. He was the leading radio personality in the United States. As Frosini put it, my father would be a tough act to follow.

Here's Dad's story, told in his own inimitable way.

CHAPTER THREE

THE FACE ON THE SUBWAY FLOOR

It was a pleasure to hear your voice again, while your son was on vacation. I have to tell you now, Mr. Gambling, I never did follow those healthy exercises you were promoting. I ate Baby Ruth candy bars all the while. And I still weigh only 120 pounds.

(Mrs.) Georgette Klauber
RD 2, Sussex, N.J.

JOHN B: I certainly did not want to follow in my father's profession. His name was John, but without a middle initial, and he was a civil engineer employed by the university town of Cambridge, England, to oversee road-building. This provided him with professional status but very low pay. His real love, which might have been his profession if he'd been able to live by it, was magic—sleight-of-hand. He did not attempt the big illusions, such as sawing a woman in half or levitating a member of the audience. His were mainly card tricks. He had the face and manner for it: tall, thin, with a marvelous bristling mustache, waxed to a fierce point, and an upright, almost aristocratic, bearing that commanded attention. You could not ignore him on stage. And he would not bend to the fads of a changing world. He came to visit us one year in the 1930s and I can still see him on a trip to Jones Beach with Mother. He sat stiffly under a beach umbrella in his black wool suit; his jacket was off but he would not remove his tie.

He drafted me as his stage assistant when I was about ten. I brought on a small table with the wire stand that held a deck of cards, or removed the dozens of colored

silk squares he pulled out of an empty cigarette case. I
worked with him one winter night, in New Market, about
fifteen miles from home. It took hours on the frozen road,
and the coachman and groom had to put nails on the
horses' hooves to keep them from sliding. His fee for the
full hour of legerdemain was ten shillings, about $2.40
in those days.

The shows were not fun for me. What turned me
against magic were Father's constant demands. I would
be out playing with friends in the street, and he'd call,
"Boy! Come in here," to demonstrate a new trick and
gauge my reaction to it. I felt he never gave me any time
for myself. He believed a boy should think only about
work—no time for pleasure. The most important thing
was to make your way in the world. He was a good man
and ambitious for me; while he was adept at sleight-of-
hand, he was certainly clumsy in handling a child. I recall
rushing home from school with my end-of-term report. I
stood second in the class, and I was understandably
elated. He glanced over the report and said, "Why weren't
you first?" That took the heart out of me. Next term, I
was near the bottom.

Cambridge County School was the equivalent of a prep
school in America. I don't believe there were any free
schools. Father paid six pounds (about $29) a term; it
was a lot of money at the turn of the century, and he had
to scrimp for it. The masters wore academic gowns in
class, but only the headmaster was permitted to cane us.
For major crimes, such as smoking, he laid on ten of the
best. Charles James Hoolihan Child had been a minister;
while you were waiting to be caned, you were in limbo.
And tortured with truly Victorian ingenuity. A closet behind his desk held about a dozen supple canes. While
you stood, trembling, he would take one out, heft it, then
put it back. It was obviously too light for your crime.
After many tries, he found the proper instrument, and
then he would say, "All right, boy—touch your toes."

There were some compensating pleasures at school. I
was on the second-string football [soccer] team. The
skills of cricket eluded me, but I batted and ran with

fervor. Last year, I visited Cambridge and made a point of booking at the hotel that overlooks the common. From my window, I watched the boys at play, and it was still cricket and football. Little had changed in the sixty years since I had been one of them.

Father had plans for me. A relative managed a nursery in Norwich. Father must have thought: I'll start a nursery for my boy, and when he grows up, he'll have his own business; he'll never have to work for the civil service— he'll be his own boss. He yanked me out of school when I was thirteen—I never finished the Fourth Form—on the theory that a boy who hadn't learned enough to take him through life by the age of thirteen was a moron who never would learn anymore. I was apprenticed to the nurseryman at four shillings and sixpence a week, less than a dollar.

I resisted it. I could not see how character was built and the soul was gratified by rising at dawn to dig and weed. But, here, too, there were compensations. Automobiles were rich men's toys in those days. I acquired a much older friend, a rakish fellow who took autos out to prospective customers for inspection. He chugged by at 10 o'clock; I'd hop in and together we bounced around the countryside, admiring the natural wonders. He returned me to work at four, and I rode home on my bicycle at six. Until Father heard of it.

He sent me up north to Glasgow, to another nursery which I also hated. I transferred myself to one on the coast southwest of Glasgow, near Ayr. I was about three miles from Prestwick, a small seaside resort before the age of the airplane; during World War II it exploded into a giant American Air Force base. On the other side of Prestwick was the pretty hamlet of Troon. I worked from dawn to dusk, but enjoyed it because I was near resort towns and there was plenty of fun after work. Well, even in those days, you couldn't spend time with girls without spending money. After I'd paid for my room and board, I was broke. So I hocked my bicycle in Kilmarnock and informed Father my bike had been stolen—would he send me another one? The practice of magic had turned

him into a profound skeptic; he wrote to the chief of the
constabulary at Kilmarnock, asking if I'd reported a stolen
bicycle. I must have forgotten that detail, because Father
wrote back: "Just walk." For the rest of my sentence in
Scotland, I did. And with every yard I trudged, I detested
the nursery more and more.

(Here's a bit of irony: Some years before I retired, I
looked around for a business that would keep me busy
and outdoors. The man who had been tending the lawn
and garden at my house in Old Field, L.I., suggested the
ideal business for my purpose—a nursery! And he talked
me into it. I bought some land at a town nearby, Mt.
Sinai, and opened a professional operation with him as
manager. I lost money every year. Even though I used
"Rambling With Gambling" to sell my stock by mail every
spring. The azaleas and rhododendrons were of excellent
quality, but we couldn't compete with the cheaper supermarket product. When I retired from radio, I couldn't
afford the losses anymore, so I sold the fourteen acres.
Fortunately, Long Island real estate had increased in
value enough for me to break even on the whole deal.
So I don't hate the nursery business anymore.)

For some reason, which escapes me at the moment, I
had always wanted to go to sea. It was a romantic notion
that stayed with me all through my teens. I had sense
enough not to run away as a cabin boy or ordinary sea-
man; I'd had enough of slave labor. I wanted to be an
officer. The sinking of the *Titanic*, April 15, 1912, clari-
fied my vision. I would learn wireless telegraphy and save
the lives of thousands of people. Somehow, I persuaded
Father that the brand-new science of the "wireless" had
more of a future than trimming tulip bulbs. In the fall
of 1913, he sent me off to the British School of Telegraphy in London. Without a bicycle.

By July 1914, I'd passed the necessary examinations
and was classified as a duly-qualified wireless operator.
Next month, Britain declared war on Germany. On
August 10, I enlisted in the British Navy as Chief Petty
Officer (Telegraphist) by upping my age one year. I still
had visions of heroism: with my rare skills, I would no

doubt be assigned on the flagship of Admiral Sir John Jellicoe, Commander-in-Chief of the Grand Fleet.

I was posted to duty on a 70-foot fishing trawler, the *Xylopia,* which had been converted to a minesweeper. The "radio room" had been the fish hold. These boats worked in teams, sweeping mines in the North Sea. It was ferociously cold in winter. At the end of three years, the only boat afloat of the six in our section was the good old *Xylopia.* The Admiralty mercifully transferred me to a merchant ship, converted to a cruiser, the *HMS Lunka.* We patrolled the coast off German West Africa. When we got a report that the Germans were camped on shore, we'd fire a few shells which they couldn't answer because they had no guns. That's the kind of war I was made for.

After demobilization I signed onto various British freighters and tankers, to the Near East. I saw the fabled skyline of New York for the first time in 1919, and discovered that an officer on an American ship made an astonishing $125 a month, twice the British scale. I switched to American-flag ships. In those days, a half-dozen passenger lines were plying the waters between Boston, New York, Savannah, and New Orleans. By 1924, I was an American citizen and chief wireless operator on the old *SS Creole* of the Morgan Line, and I was operating nicely with the young female passengers on vacation. Until I met a charmer named Rita Graubart, out of Albany. I proposed to her on the ship, and she accepted. On condition that I quit the sea—"swallow the anchor," as my mates put it. We were married in February 1925, and next day I went out to hustle for a job, preferably in New York.

I had only one marketable skill—wireless telegraphy. I sniffed out the few land-based opportunities for this skill. Radio was still a new and little-understood marvel. It was only twenty-six years since Marconi's "wireless" telegraph equipment had been installed on three British battleships. By 1907, Lee De Forest was demonstrating his "Audion" in experimental broadcasts from the top floor of a building at Fourth Avenue and 19th Street, in New York. WJZ had opened in a shack in Newark, N.J., in October 1921, and achieved national fame by the first broadcast of the World Series: Giants vs. Yankees.

In that same town, L. Bamberger's department store had partitioned off a corner of its sporting goods department for a "studio" as a publicity gimmick. On Washington's Birthday, February 22, 1922, the studio engineer, Jack Poppele, put an Al Jolson record of "April Showers" on a Victrola, set a microphone next to its big horn—and WOR made its debut on the air. The transmitter was a thriftily reconditioned 250-watter that had been used by Lee De Forest in his experiments. Surely there was some opening in New York for a 28-year-old newlywed who had already spent ten years sending and receiving radio signals, through all the hazards of storm and war.

I heard that WEAF had paid Will Rogers the incredible sum of $1,000 for a single performance, so I tried there first. I applied at their studio at 195 Broadway, headquarters of the giant American Telephone and Telegraph. A pleasant young man with slicked-back hair and a rather excited voice by the name of Graham McNamee interviewed me. He told me, very nicely and kindly, that he didn't think I was quite suited for an announcer's job. Well, I knew that.

Luck and coincidence now combined with such incredible timing that I felt Someone up high was guiding me like a puppet on a string. The former service man for the radio equipment on the Morgan Line ships was Seth Gamblin—Gambling without the g. He was an engineer at WOR's Newark operation with Jack Poppele. WOR had just opened a studio in New York, at Chickering Hall, West 57th Street, because most of the performers who clustered in New York were reluctant to make the trek across the river to Newark to work without pay. Poppele needed a licensed "wireless" operator to work there. Seth took me to see Jack in the transmitting station, a little shack on the roof of Bamberger's store. WOR was now up to 500 watts.

Poppele wasted no time. My most important qualification was my license. "I'll put you on probation," he said. "Thirty a week, take it or leave it."

I took it. This was less than my salary on the SS *Creole*, but Rita was making $40 a week as a secretary at Columbia University. I had swallowed the anchor at last. The historic date was March 8, 1925, only a week and a half after we were married.

The studio was dinky indeed. It was about 15 by 20 feet. Another room, half this size, was partitioned into a control room and an office. The receptionist and program director worked here. Since most of the would-be performers were looking for glory or publicity, the reception room was always overflowing. I had to dodge among the sopranos and fiddlers to reach my rack of controls.

A loudspeaker in the office relayed the show from the studio, which was furnished in Bamberger's off-the-floor specials: living-room carpet, heavy red damask drapes, overstuffed sofa, a table, and Baldwin grand piano. When a guest sat down in that sofa, he couldn't get up easily— I had to carry the mike-stand to him.

Seth, Jack, and I were the engineering staff; two of us had to be on duty while WOR broadcast. Of course, we weren't on twenty-four hours a day. The day began with Bernarr Macfadden's calisthenics, 6:30 to 8 A.M. (he had WOR's largest audience); we continued from 10 to 11; 2:30 to 4 and 6 to 10 at night. And never on Sundays. Since I was the new man, I got the 6:30 shift.

On my second day, Poppele decided I might as well announce for Macfadden, too. I had never spoken into a microphone in my life—but I didn't want to confuse Poppele by telling him that. Nobody worked from written scripts. My first words, haltingly improvised, were: "Good morning, ladies and gentlemen. This is radio station WOR, New York, signing on at exactly 6:30 A.M. We now bring you Mister Bernarr Macfadden, the distinguished expert on health. . . ."

In those days, everybody was distinguished. My wife picked up a copy of the New York *Graphic* and found a full-page picture of me: "The distinguished announcer, John B. Gambling, now announcing Bernarr Macfadden's show." I discovered that Macfadden owned the *Graphic* and paid WOR for the exercise-show time in order to promote the paper. His magazines, *Physical Culture* and *True Story,* had a circulation of several million. My wife threw the rest of the *Graphic* away; it was the most lurid scandal-sheet in town. The quality of its writing and pictures compared favorably with the "underground" papers of today's Greenwich Village. The *Graphic* surpassed them, however, in one technique: composite photographs of sensational sex scandals. The editors would pose models for the camera, then substitute the heads of the actual personalities involved.

I liked Macfadden. He must have been in his late fifties then, slender, wiry, with tremendous energy and piercing eyes that went through you like a dentist's drill. He was a fanatic, of course, on diet and physical fitness. But he was doing headstands and handsprings, and jumping 2,500 feet with a parachute into the Hudson on his eighty-third birthday, so there may have been some substance in his eccentric crusades. He practiced what he preached. He forced all the employees of his publications into daily bends and stretches; no excuses accepted unless accompanied by a doctor's certification. I recall the studio door locked shut at Chickering Hall one morning, and I couldn't find a watchman to open it. Macfadden acted instantly. He ran down to the street to pick up a 2 by 4 plank from a construction site. "All right, everybody get hold of it!" he ordered. I complied, puzzled, and so did one of his daughters, who was on the show that day. We bashed the door in.

Bernarr had five daughters, whose names all began with B—Beverly, Beulah, Brenda, Barbara, and Belinda. They'd also do handsprings and exercises for the benefit of the *Graphic* photographer. He'd bring them around on Saturday, and I'd write a few lines for each to read:

"I enjoy these exercises so much because they help keep my figure trim. My boyfriends say I'm fit as a fiddle, and you can be, too." (Giggle)

The three-piece orchestra (later four) provided marches and waltzes to pep up the devotees creaking beside their radios. It was fifteen minutes of exercise, alternating with fifteen minutes of music, for one and a half hours. Macfadden sent out, on request, an elaborate diagrammed chart of thirty-six exercises he'd devised. He went through all of them, from (1) "Deep Breathing—Raise arms high over the head, up on the toes" through (18) "Russian Dance—Squat, thrusting left leg forward, placing hands on floor at sides, alternating with right leg" to (36) "Bicycle Ride—Go through the motions of pedaling bicycle upside down." I became exhausted just watching. Some listeners claimed they did the Russian Dance with earphones on.

After two weeks, I was raised to $35. Six months later, Macfadden phoned to say that he wouldn't be in that morning. I called Poppele at the transmitter in Newark: "What do we do?"

"You have the exercise chart?"

"Yes."

"Do you know the routine?"

"Sure."

"Go to the microphone and do the routine."

> POPPELE: Within a few minutes, the phone started to ring in Newark: Women wanted to know where that beautiful voice came from. Macfadden had the gruff call of an army drill sergeant. John had a clear baritone voice, plus something we did not have on the air: dignity and precise diction, the result of his British background. No "toidy-toid street" roughness. The resonance of his voice seemed to penetrate the mike and come right out in the speakers at home.

JOHN B: After a few weeks, Macfadden abandoned the show to devote full-time to his publishing empire. Since he was his own sponsor, this left a great hole in the morning. I volunteered to fill in with music and chatter until the station could find a permanent replacement— at no extra charge. Rita was not happy about this: "Why do you want to knock yourself out so early every morning for nothing?" I felt something would come of it.

Something had to—I needed money. We were living

in a one-room apartment on 122nd Street near Riverside
Drive, so Rita could be near her work at Columbia. We
had one of those beds that folded out of a closet; if the
bed was down, we couldn't entertain any guests. When I
left in the morning, she feared the bed would suddenly
fly up into the closet, and she'd be stuck there. Another
apartment was indicated.

Substituting for Macfadden was like a Marx Brothers
movie—"A Day at the Gym." I was all alone in the studio;
the second engineer was nursing the transmitter in Newark. I'd come in early, check the equipment, warm it up,
alert the man in New Jersey, check the time. At 6:30,
I'd dash over to the mike and deliver the exercises. "Get
out of bed . . . get your charts . . . come on, smile! . . .
Ready, one, two, three, four . . ." I ad-libbed with the
orchestra, and while they were tootling, I'd run into the
control room to check the volume. Then out again to call,
"Hands on hips, side-straddle hop!" The orchestra was a
lot of fun, but I had to keep an eye on Frosini, the accordionist. His ancient vaudeville gags were often too gamy
for radio. In those days, everything was very proper and
straight—you couldn't even say "lousy." As soon as I
detected an eager twitch in his eyelids, I choked him off
by ordering, "Play, boys."

After three months, I picked up my first sponsor, Col-
gate toothpaste. The full hour and a half, with a commercial every fifteen minutes. What cautious pioneers we
were. The sponsor wanted me to be photographed in a
gym suit, doing those exercises. Well, I was young and
supple, but I just wasn't up to those exercises at that
hour. I couldn't even get into posing position for half of
them. I was photographed standing in the "ready position," and the full exercises were drawn in outline, as a
series of dashes. I sat on a high stool, keeping time and
cheering the drowsy muscle-stretchers with old British
Navy jokes. Occasionally, I'd sing along in my busted
baritone—"Pack Up Your Troubles in Your Old Kit Bag."

I received a great deal of favorable response in letters,
mainly from plump women seeking advice on how to lose
weight. I replied: I am not qualified to give personal

advice, consult your physician. I also delivered the correct time at fifteen-minute intervals, to get my listeners off to work. Gradually I worked in weather reports and news, extracted from the morning papers.

I would announce that I was reading from, say, *The New York Times,* and the opinions expressed were not necessarily those of the management of WOR. Next morning, I'd read from the *Tribune,* and on the day after, I'd give the *American* a break. We never paid for the news, and the papers never objected; I suppose they welcomed my broadcasts as free publicity instead of piracy.

WOR forgot all about replacing me and the show was retitled *The Musical Clock.*

In addition to all this, I was WOR's daytime announcer. *Clock* finished at 8. One day, Joe Barnett, the station manager, asked me to keep going till 10. If I felt good, I'd read ten or fifteen minutes; if I was tired, I'd cut it down to three minutes.

Gradually the station filled in that morning time with programs such as the McCann Pure Food Hour. I was announcer for that one, too. Alfred W. McCann was a pioneer in protecting consumers from food adulteration. He was encouraging and helpful, working on my diction and pace. He dubbed me Uncle John on the air, and that name stuck with me a long time.

ALFRED MCCANN, JR.: John was even the co-defendant in a million-dollar libel suit, brought against my father. The case was thrown out of court in 1930. After his death in 1931, WOR asked me to carry on the show. I was only twenty-one, studying at Georgetown University; I'd planned to become a sportswriter or a restaurateur. Well, John took me by the hand, literally coddled me; he did fifty, fifty-five minutes of the hour until I got my bearings. We worked together for sixteen years. Last year, when I celebrated my fortieth anniversary on WOR, he took me aside and said, "I can tell you now, Al. I never thought you'd make it."

JOHN B.: My son's middle name is a token of my appre-

ciation for Al McCann. (When I told my audience that
we had christened the baby John Alfred Gambling, one
good listener wrote me indignantly: "Do you look forward
to the day when your son goes to college and carries a
suitcase with the initials JAG?")

I lost my British accent quickly. The process had begun
as soon as I hit the American freighters. To the tough
Yanks I was the "Limey," the kid with the highfalutin'
Cambridge accent. On land, my New Yorkization occasionally befuddled the natives. I dropped into a drugstore
on Broadway to ask, "Have you any hair oil?"

The druggist, inspecting me critically over his steel-rim
glasses, grunted, "You can't git that here."

That baffled me. "No hair oil?"

"You heard me," he snapped. "Scram!"

"Now, look here. I merely want a small bottle of oil
to put on my hair."

"My God," he sighed. "I thought you said *heroin*."

I'm a verbal chameleon now. When I visit Cambridge,
my accent in a few days turns to high-Cantabrigian.

By 1926, WOR was crying for more room. We moved
to the fifth floor of the brand-new skyscraper at 1440
Broadway. This was the Pre-air-conditioned Age, when
perspiration was 90 percent of inspiration. Luckily, the
plaster in the studio didn't dry out for six months: the
walls stayed damp and cool that summer. They were
covered with brown monk's cloth, presumably to improve
acoustics, but I felt like a cat being drowned in a big
cloth bag. Two table fans helped blow the hot air around.
We couldn't use them while a show was on, of course,
because of the racket they made. And Sunday was a day
of respite. When we came in Monday, the studio smelled
like the hold of a Malay schooner crossing the equator. To
make life more uncomfortable, we had orders to wear
tuxedos on the evening shows. I'd take two or three spare
collars along. Why dress up when there was no studio
audience? Well, the musical talent liked to wear formal
clothes and our rival, WEAF, wore them, so we had to
do it. Radio was reaching for "class." All performances
were live; recordings were considered cheap and de-
meaning.

This classy studio was about 20 by 30 feet, just off the elevators; it had two windows and two mikes. For individual speakers, lecturers, poets, we used a small compartment in one corner, the size of a telephone booth. One man, who had an obsessive love for poetry by Kipling, was kept on tap as a fill-in. When we needed to cover ten minutes while the orchestra set up, he'd recite "Gunga Din" or "Boots." One afternoon we forgot about him and he marched right on, all through the afternoon, with "Boots-boots-boots, movin' up and down again. . . ."

An afternoon program consisted usually of a soprano, tenor, contralto or baritone—not necessarily in that sequence, but all unpaid. If a singer didn't show, because of a sore throat or a demanding Fourth of July, I filled in with a travel talk, describing the enthralling ports I'd explored on my voyages. Or I called in a talented pianist who was also an announcer, Edward S. Breck. I'd introduce him in a "concert recital" of fifteen minutes of Chopin or Liszt. Followed by the "renowned English virtuoso, Sally Hardscrabble"—and Breck would play fifteen minutes of Arthur Sullivan's operettas. He could play on and on in any style, any period.

The boys in the orchestra had their own little games. I used to read birthday announcements every day. Rastus and Frosini liked to sneak phony names into the list; if I wasn't alert, I'd find myself announcing the birthdays of Holly Moses or Freda Slaves.

The studio overlooked an old hotel that has since been mercifully torn down. We'd peer out occasionally, just to keep in touch with humanity. Once, I spotted a particularly human couple in the hotel. My interest piqued Breck, who cut his Brahms concerto in half and introduced me in a "Sunny Italy" travel talk—so he could view the scene himself. I cut Italy to two minutes and brought back Breck as "Jacques Bastille from Montreal." Then it was my turn at the window.

Radio was relaxed in those days: low pressure, friendly, more fun. Little money but lots of laughs. WOR's farm editor was another great character, Joe Bier, who'd started in life as a singer. Much of New York State and New Jersey was farmland then, so Joe came on from

5:30 to 6 A.M. to read the market reports for grain, poultry, and produce, plus up-to-the-minute prices of hogs in
Chicago. Most of his energy was expended in trying to
break me up at the mike. He and Johnny Cook, our engineer, once began to undress me in the middle of my
exercise calls. I didn't laugh, even when they pulled my
pants down. I kicked one of them in the shins and his
eerie "*Yoww!*" was all the audience heard. Joe fell apart
when anyone went through the motions of playing a
violin; I don't understand why. When he sang "Road to
Mandalay," I pantomimed a gypsy fiddler and he collapsed in hysterical laughter.

Jack Byrne, who was added as Cook's assistant, pulled
a lulu on me. As I began to read my 8 A.M. news from
the *Tribune,* he wandered in to shake my hand. I greeted
him with a nod and shook the friendly paw—it was full
of glue! I needed a few minutes to untangle my fingers
when I turned a page. But I stuck to my job.

I used to read the entire list of McCann Food Hour
sponsors at the opening of the show. They were lettered
on a large cardboard, which I held in both hands. Young
Al would sneak in behind me and balance a paper cup—
filled with ice water—on my head. It was paralyzing.

> ALFRED MCCANN, JR.: One gag really cracked John
> up. He had sent out for coffee and Danish and
> scrambled eggs—he was a chain-coffee drinker—
> and the waiter carried the tray into the studio.
> (Radio was very elegant then.) John was talking
> about natural food coloring as he whisked the
> damask napkin off the tray. There, on the white
> porcelain, nestled a cluster of dog droppings! Arti-
> ficial, of course.

*

JOHN B.: We moved up to the twenty-fourth floor of 1440
early in 1927. The layout was elaborate and roomy, yet
the unforeseen hazards, the sneaky little gremlins, were
again everywhere.

In the never-ending search for "class," the reception
room had been decorated with overstuffed sofas, and the

largest studio was festooned with imported crystal chandeliers. It could accommodate a forty-piece symphony. At the first rehearsals, the conductor detected a mysterious Oriental tinkle in the Beethoven. The crystal pendants were vibrating like tuning forks. Down came the chandeliers.

Our elaborate facilities became the nursery for the Columbia Broadcasting System. I was one of the attendants at the birth. In January 1927, a group of visionaries, led by Arthur Judson, who managed opera and concert stars, and Major J. Andrew White, who dangled a pincenez at the end of a black ribbon, formed a network to compete with NBC. They lined up fifteen stations, north to Providence, R.I., and west to Iowa. They had one fundamental problem: no studio or transmitter in New York City. So they sublet studio space and transmitter time from WOR: Monday, Wednesday, and Friday nights, 9 to 11, and Sunday, 3 to 5 and 9 to 11. WOR became the key station in the network. The big splash debut was set for Sunday night, September 18, 1927; a four-hour extravaganza with one hundred artists, symphonic and dance orchestras, a variety show, and a Metropolitan Opera company in a full-length performance of *The King's Henchman* by Deems Taylor. Another fundamental problem arose: the new switching equipment did not arrive in time to be connected, and the program was scheduled to emanate from four studios. We did it with "patch cords," like an old-style telephone switchboard. To switch from one studio to another, one engineer stood up, pulled his cord and yelled "Cut!" and an engineer at the other end of the control racks plugged in his cord. Then he yelled "Cut!" for the next switch. It worked. Columbia later got enough money together to buy its own station and transmitter and severed its connection with WOR in September 1929.

It was time for innovation because the industry was starting from scratch. In 1927, I came up with the concept of the first Mr. and Mrs. radio show. And the Mrs. wasn't my own—Rita was still typing for the profs at Columbia University. My radio wife was a very clever actress, quick and sharp on the ad-libs. It was fifteen minutes of chatter, sponsored by the *New York American* to promote its classified ads. I had a five-and-dime-store cup, saucer, and spoon. I opened by rattling the spoon against the cup: "Good morning, darling . . ." She would improvise into "We really need a new dining-room set."

"I tell you what we'll do," I shot back. "We'll look into the classified ads of the *New York American*. There's bound to be something for sale." I read over a few of their ads, then ten or fifteen minutes of news from the *American*. I'd rattle our props again and she'd come up with, "The maid is leaving to marry her old boyfriend in Virginia." So we'd get back to those ads to find a maid.

I couldn't break her up. Once I suggested, "I'm getting tired of our children—isn't it time we had another one?"

She came back with, "No, we're going to have a puppy instead. And we're going to find it in the classified ads."

After six months, the *American* got tired of our act and sponsored me in fifteen minutes of straight news. That was great. I'd been reading it without pay.

By 1928 I was making $100 a week, a grand sum for those times. Rita felt secure enough to quit her secretarial position at Columbia, although she did cling to some part-time work. And I was becoming a celebrity. I picked up the *New York World*'s Sunday supplement of November 10, 1928, and discovered that I had arrived at last. There I was on the cover, drawn in black-crayon style, with the caption "Uncle John, the popular director of WOR's early morning gym class." Elated, I bought six copies and hurried into the subway to carry them to my wife.

My euphoria was swiftly deflated. On the floor of the train lay dozens of Uncle Johns and hundreds of feet were tramping over me. The first thing New Yorkers did with the Sunday *World* was throw away the supplement. Well, no matter. I was now successful enough to let my wife work only part-time.

CHAPTER FOUR

BLOOPERS AND BLOOMERS AND THE CAT'S MEOW

He had little canaries singing.
Mama would shlep us out of bed
and scream, "John Gambling
says it's late already. The canaries are singing!" When he
played the march music, Mama
knew we had to be finished with
breakfast and on the way to
school.

Arnold Fine, Columnist
The Jewish Press,
July 19, 1968

The Musical Clock woke up sponsors, too. The Illinois
Meat Company of Chicago wanted to break into the New
York market with its corned-beef hash. Since its local dis-
tributor was an exercise fan, he nominated my show to
promote the hash. The company bought our four-piece
orchestra, one and a half hours of time, five days a week
—and me—for only $900. The product was labeled
Broadcast Brand Corned Beef Hash, and it became a win-
ner. We still eat it, and I'm not being paid for this plug.
I know of only one person who didn't like it. He sent a
card, care of my sponsor: "Dear John, I bought a can of
Broadcast Brand hash and then I bought a can of Red
Heart dog food. I took one look, threw away the hash, and
ate the dog food." Fortunately, the sponsor was a man of
humor—he didn't can me.

Another product, a condensed milk, frankly revolted
me. It was a clean, healthy milk, I'm sure, but I had a
peculiar aversion: It smelled like a moist baby. For a
sound-effect, I bought a little toy cow that sounded like

moooo-ooow . . . mooo-oooooow. Long-drawn and very
realistic. This became Nellie the Cow. I'd ask Nellie how
she liked this brand milk, and I'd manipulate that cow
until she mooed in a positive rapture. This prop stimu-
lated the owner of an amusement park in Staten Island
into an idea for a publicity tie-in: a picnic for Nellie! At
his park.

I opposed the whole notion from the start. He rented a
poor, sway-backed cow, who was old enough to have
started the Chicago fire. Our publicity genius wanted me
to lead her down Broadway to the Battery and put her on
the ferry to Staten Island. I balked at that, but agreed to
pose for pictures "milking" her at the park. In September
1929, some farmer was hired to pull and push that poor
animal from City Hall down Broadway. She blocked traffic and in the confusion climbed up the steps of the old
Standard Oil building in the financial district . . . in the
middle of a bull market. I took my car on the ferry to
meet the instigator of all this nonsense at the Staten Island end. We were late, so I speeded up to fifty. Sure
enough, a policeman stopped me and ad-libbed the usual
question, "Where do you think you're going?"

"To my cow's picnic," I answered, quite seriously.

This irritated him; but after he saw my driver's license
he murmured he heard my show regularly and "it's a
pleasure to meet you" as he wrote out the summons.

At the park, drinks and food were on the house. The
photographers pressed for a shot of Uncle John milking
Nellie. I was perspiring and exasperated; there was a
smile on my face but black fear in my heart. Nellie was
skittish and kicking, and obviously too old to give milk
even if I had known which valve to turn. I faked it, but
the cow actually worked—and this time the drink was on
me. All over my newly pressed suit.

Next day I paid the $25 speeding fine in court and
vowed never to play stooge to any animal again. A
newspaper headline caught the scene nicely: "Man Who
Says 'Good Morning' to Thousands Says 'Good Morning,
Judge.' "

Sponsors began to crowd around with every imaginable

product. I felt I was a guest in the listener's home—I did
not want to intrude early in the morning with ads for
cold cures and laxatives. I was able to talk our sales department out of these ads; in later years I secured a
clause in my contract that permitted me to reject any
product I considered unsuitable. I felt personally respon-
sible for the validity of all claims made on my show.

I even had ads from the Long Island Railroad, which
in those far-gone days was actually looking for customers.
By this time I was riding in from my summer home in
Massapequa, and changing at Jamaica, so I had an opportunity to test the product every morning. It was
prompt, safe, and clean. On my twenty-fifth anniversary
celebration, Harry Hershfield, good friend and peerless
raconteur, remembered my efforts on behalf of the railroad with this story:

A commuter was injured by an unexpected jolt of a
train; as he lay on the platform waiting for the ambu-
lance, he groaned in great pain. The attendant arrived
after an hour and asked, "Where do you want us to take
you?"

"Take me anywhere," the commuter moaned. "Just
don't make me change at Jamaica!"

My heart went out to one sponsor, Peter Chambers. He
and his wife, enthusiastic fans of my show, came to an
anniversary celebration in the 1940s, in a small theater
off Times Square. Peter was an excitable Greek with a
neat little mustache like the man on a wedding cake; his
wife, Lillian, had a Clara Bow mouth. She told me later
that all they had eaten for dinner that evening was a bowl
of cereal. They operated a small Mom-and-Pop fur shop,
one flight up, on 42nd Street near Sixth Avenue, where
they sold inexpensive furs such as rabbit and muskrat.

That night, the Chamberses decided my audience was
the type they wanted to attract to their store. I did my
best to discourage them. They were practically broke, and
I did not think I or anybody could sell furs at 7 in the
morning. They persisted. I persuaded WOR to give them
a special deal; instead of the thirteen-week minimum,
they bought in for a five-week trial. Three spots at $50

each; $150 a week was a lot of money when you're eating
cereal for dinner. That day, he insisted I come down to
the fur district to meet his suppliers. Excited and bubbling with enthusiasm, he walked me around 26th and
30th Streets, between Sixth and Seventh, and all the way
he yelled up to the lofts and at people on the street, "This
is John Gambling—WOR—710 on the dial!" People came
out of the buildings to shake his hand and mine.

The commercials made him a quick success, much to
my surprise. Chambers moved up from let-out muskrat to
mink, but never moved the store from that little place on
42nd Street. Mr. and Mrs. Chambers passed on several
years ago, but I will always remember those two people,
who had more faith in me than I had in myself.

*

There was drama and immediacy in the early days of
radio, because all of it was broadcast live; this also had
its disadvantages. Broadcasts originating outside the
studio ("remotes") required special equipment. It was
rather primitive: a microphone, amplifier, huge wet B-
batteries to supply power, and yards and yards of wire.
WOR had only one set of this gear. I would lug the amplifier and mike in one hand, the B-batteries in the other,
with the wire coiled around my neck. To cover the celebration of a New Year's Eve, I'd do the remotes dressed in
a tuxedo: the Roseland ballroom, from 8 to 9; disconnect,
drag the equipment to the Paramount Hotel, hook up
again for a show 10 to 11; and set it all up again in
Times Square for the raucous welcome at midnight. With
every move, the B-batteries leaked acid on my formal
trousers. A few hours after I stowed away my remote
equipment, I had to go on for my regular show at 6:45
A.M.

New Year's Eve broadcasts were a special kind of nightmare because the revelers were so high on Prohibition
booze. As they sang "Auld Lang Syne" I was on the ballroom floor at my controls, and tipsy women were certain
to spill what was called port wine on my white dress
shirt. And the language those ladies whispered into the

orchestra's mike as they danced by, made ex-sailor Gambling wince. I stood guard every minute to switch them off; we had no tape-recording technique to "beep" them out the way engineers do today.

The station was in a constant scramble for interviews with celebrities, any famous name, even if he or she had nothing to say. I gained some notoriety for ingenuity by my "exclusive" with Queen Marie of Rumania. She visited America in October 1926; WOR made plans to get in on this publicity junket by broadcasting a special program for her. At the last minute, we learned she would be unable to hear it. She would be on a train speeding between Philadelphia and New York when our program was scheduled. What to do? We had no way as yet to broadcast from a moving train, and I didn't know whether she spoke English anyhow. I was dispatched to board the train in Philadelphia with a receiver and aerial so that she could hear our broadcast and comment on the wonders of WOR radio.

I explained my mission to the stolid Irish stationmaster in Philadelphia; he made it clear that no S.O.B. could get on this train with "all them funny black boxes and wires." When the train stopped, I prevailed on the State Department man in charge to let me on. I set up my equipment and aerial and picked up the opening of the show from New York: the Rumanian National Anthem. All clear and beautiful. And then I learned Her Majesty was taking a nap! She woke up halfway through the finale: an enthralling speech entitled "The Queen as Passenger," delivered by Captain Hubert E. Hartley, captain of the *Leviathan,* the ship on which she'd come to America. (We certainly touched all bases.)

I explained to Her Majesty how this complicated broadcasting system had been set up, and since I didn't know how well she spoke English, I enunciated slowly and carefully, in words of one syllable, as if to a baby. She thanked me in a beautiful Oxford accent: "It was wonderful. I never dreamed that radio could be heard on a moving train." And she gave me her hand to kiss. After having crawled all over the train to set up, I was as grimy as the man shoveling coal into the engine. Reluctantly, I took her hand into my blackened paw—and shook it. This rare scene was dutifully reported in the newspapers—we couldn't broadcast any of it. Later, I expressed my chagrin to WOR's president, Al McCosker, that the Queen's English was better than mine. "You damn fool," he answered. "Didn't you know she's part of the British Royal family?"

Because I worked alone on most remotes, as engineer-announcer, I had to think faster than the speed of sound. In 1929, I broadcast the dedication of a carillon in St. Thomas Church on Fifth Avenue. I was warned there would be a two-minute lag in the ceremonies, but I could fill that easily enough. I dragged my equipment up high into the tower. The two minutes stretched on and on . . . and there I was marooned. You can't tell gags in a church. I launched into a comparison of the architecture of St. Thomas with that of King's College Chapel and Trinity Hall Chapel at Cambridge—for twenty-five minutes. I didn't know much beyond the difference between a Tudor tower and a Gothic arch. The minister, nevertheless, received several letters from parishioners, praising the wide knowledge of architecture I'd displayed.

Another, more unfortunate, brush with the church occurred in 1930: a rebroadcast of a speech by Pope Pius XI, direct from Rome. I was called on to introduce this historic event; the station's highest echelons and dignitaries of the church assembled in the control room and studios. I had to finish at exactly 11 o'clock, when the Pope would speak. I was a little shaky, since I had absolutely no knowledge of Italian or Latin. I ended my intro exactly on the nose with ". . . and now, ladies and gentlemen, the voice of His Holiness, Pipe Po-us." This certainly ranks with the classic blooper attributed to Harry Von Zell, who once introduced our thirty-first President as "Hoobert Herver."

The most unsettling fact about live radio was—once you committed a verbal blunder, you couldn't call it back for correction. Wanamaker's bought time on my show when the store was at Broadway and 8th Street. The ad manager would send me the full-page advertisement from the *Herald-Tribune*, with the items checked for mention on the air. This procedure worked nicely for months, until I received a page of women's underwear. I'd given a long discourse earlier that morning on why I liked to investigate the background of products on my show. This is what came out of my listeners' Majestic table receiver: "Ladies, this morning we're going to talk about bloomers. Now, as you know, I always like to delve into the things I talk about. . . ."

This became known as Gambling's classic bloomer.

I interviewed hundreds of celebrities, in the studio and on remotes, from Sir Thomas Lipton, the tea merchant and eternal loser of yacht races (he refused to be photographed with any woman anywhere), to movie star Marion Davies (rather quiet and shy), to Gypsy Rose Lee. The former burlesque peeler was the most literate of all. Her wit was keen, she was quick and never at a loss for a reply. I spoke to her at Madison Square Garden, in a tiny room off the arena, just before her entrance atop an elephant in the Ringling Brothers circus.

The most intriguingly sexy voice belonged to Lita Gray Chaplin, Charlie's former wife. I worked a food-promotion show with her in Union City, N.J., in 1929. She had a sultry beauty and a provocative voice, pitched as low as Charles Boyer's. Lita handed out dried dates to all. Women were so stunned by her beauty, they picked up the fruit in their white cloth gloves, oblivious to the fact that the gooey stuff was ruining the fabric.

At the end of the 1920s, WOR presented a weekly one-hour playlet, set in a rural village: *The Main Street Sketches*. There was no continuing story, only a series of comic situations and characters. The hero, Luke Higgins, was played by Don Carney, who ran Uncle Don's children's show in the afternoon. Members of the staff were expected to pitch in and play two or three parts. I was a guest occasionally, playing myself as a visitor in town. I reached into my collection of jokes to enliven the occasion. The sketches were thrown together by the station's program director, Leonard Cox, page by page. He worked in a small office, assisted by a bottle of Scotch; a messenger would bring us the results while the show was on the air, one page at a time. The players crowded around the mike to read from the single copy. The haphazard humor of *Main Street Sketches* became wildly popular. Fans gathered neighbors and friends together on Monday nights to listen in. This phenomenon reappeared in the early days of television with Milton Berle's show, Tuesday night at 8.

Our unbridled success led Cox to send us out on the road as the "WOR Players" in a live hour-and-a-half variety show. He chartered a bus and took us around for benefit performances in the Brooklyn Academy of Music, Rotary clubs, churches. The show consisted of several Main Street scenes, Don Carney with a routine, and assorted instrumentalists and vocalists. I came on strong with three girls in bathing suits. Wrapped in flashy silk pajamas and a luxurious bathrobe, I'd stretch out on a settee, puff a cigarette in a long holder and order the girls through a tough workout of my radio exercises. As usual, we worked for gratis, for the greater glory of WOR and for our own egos. It was fun for a while, performing for and meeting fans whom we would otherwise never see; our wives went along for the ride. It ended when we discovered that somebody was collecting as much as $1,000 a night for the show—and pocketing it.

In these years, I was collecting jokes and squirreling them away in my files. They were corny, funny, and unashamedly aged, culled from *Collier's, Liberty, College Humor,* and my memories of English music halls. Most were contributed by listeners. My files consisted of large manila envelopes, labeled with the months of the year. On January 1, I'd pull out the January envelope; on January 31, I'd put all the slips of paper, cards, and clippings back again and start on February. Under this system, I repeated my jokes only once a year, a lot less than TV comedians do nowadays.

Radio, which appeals to the ear, depended on sound gags, just as movies and TV appeal to the eye with sight gags. "The Musical Clock" time was announced every fifteen minutes, heralded by the voice of a cuckoo. Mike Rosco, my pianist, created it with the help of fingers pressed to his lips. I created Henrietta the Hen, with my own vocal cords, to shame the late risers. In 1946, the New Jersey Poultry Owners' Association gave me a live Henrietta to promote the sale of their eggs. Unfortunately, the real hen could not cluck on cue; after photographs of the presentation, she was quietly sent back to New Jersey.

A listener sent me a little squeeze gadget that sounded like a cat. "Well," I announced, "we've now got a cat on the show—meow! meow! What shall we call the cat?" I had been in America only a short time, so I had not yet assimilated the ethnic nuances of New Yorkese. Jack Poppele used "tochus" for "thinga-mabob" or "gimmick." "I know what we'll call the cat. We'll call him Tochus!" I instantly realized, from the look of despair on Jack's face, that I had made a terrible booboo, but I had no idea what it was. I improvised desperately: "You don't like that name? Okay—how about Tojo?" "Tochus," I learned later, is Yiddish for "derriere."

I acquired a fan, possibly encouraged by these meows, who developed a strange passion for my show—a cat! Here's the bizarre tale from the Brattleboro, Vermont, *Daily Reformer:*

> As the gray dawn approaches, the cat meows, at first graciously and politely, then plaintively and finally peevishly if the radio is not turned on. If the owner persists in sleeping late, the cat gets up on a table, clawing at the dials. Our scout says he has seen the marks. When the longed-for voice of Gambling and the sound of the music fill the room, the cat purrs and assumes an air of great comfort and joy. And a beatific look covers her face.

Canaries were my longest-running gag. They even made the transition to television. The radio canary chorus was supplied by the Hartz Mountain birdseed people to promote their products. The ensemble numbered about twenty, and they were brought to the studio every morning, in little cages, by the Bird Groom, John (Hugo) Kennedy. Here they could sing into their own mike, with the orchestra or *a cappella.* After the show, Hugo packed them home to a pet shop downtown. The bird songs were cheerful; regrettably, they sang during the commercials, too. The Bird Groom stood by, hands raised like an orchestra conductor, to cajole them into silence. Once, when he was out of the studio, they warbled during a particularly serious commercial. I rolled up a newspaper and threw it toward the cages. Bull's-eye. The cages scattered as they hit the floor, and the freed birds fluttered around the studio. Chaos. In 1950, the birds sang for the last time, and I expected an avalanche of protests from bird lovers. I received only five or six letters.

Very few changes were made in the format of the morning show in the thirty-four years I operated it. A big break with tradition came in 1934. Several companies were selling records for exercise at home; you could do them anytime you were up to it, if you suffered by being rousted out early in the morning. I made a survey among close friends and listeners, and found that very few people were exercising at all. This came as a blow to me, since the show from the beginning had been based on the universal appeal of good health. I dropped the exercises, charts and all. Again, very few protests. In fact, I received some letters from listeners who frankly admitted they felt better now, less guilty, because they never had done those bends and jumps. I continued with the orchestra, the ad-lib chatter, time and news reports, and my audience kept growing. I finally had to drop the live music in 1954 after a financial hassle between the musician's union and WOR. I hated to see my friends Rastus and Froz and the others go, but the quality and variety of the recorded music was better.

1934 was also the year in which John A. made his debut. The Christmas show was not a conscious innovation; again it was something I just slid into. Sometime in 1930, after fluffing the pronunciation of several birthday names, I announced I would put 25¢, for each mistake, into a box—to be contributed to the Salvation Army at the end of the year. A good time for contributions, of course, was Christmas. From here it was a short step to inviting the Salvation Army's Cadet Choir to sing carols on the morning before Christmas. And I brought Rita on, because quite a few women wondered what my wife was like.

Each year my fluffs added up to $50 or $60. John continued this custom for a while after I retired. When I substituted on his vacation, I made a fluff and automatically reached into the desk drawer to deposit a quarter. The only thing in the box was a sheet of paper:

I O U $1.25 (crossed out)
I O U $2.50 (crossed out)
I O U $3.75

John had run out of a lot of change.

The weeks and months of radio rolled on . . . over five hundred shows a year. They were happy and productive years; some stand out as milestones.

1934: WOR's power exploded from 5,000 to 50,000 watts, reaching seven states with a population of 18 million people.

March 8, 1945: On my twentieth anniversary, Mayor Fiorello LaGuardia, the politician who harnessed perpetual motion, popped into my studio at 7 A.M. with this greeting: "As a bum commentator to a good one, I really want to congratulate you. . . . Anyone who can maintain a pleasant, cheerful program for twenty years has to be good."

1948: A WOR survey found me pulling 315,000 people out of bed every day. I didn't know whether to be proud or guilty. *Variety,* the show-business bible, rated *Rambling With Gambling* first among the top twenty daytime shows in New York. Ahead of Kate Smith, Arthur Godfrey, Phil Cook.

Arthur and I were friendly competitors for years. One month he'd be a point ahead of me in the ratings; next month I'd be one up on him. He worked for WCBS, from 6:30 to 7:45 A.M., with recorded music and chatter and his inimitable philosophy. Rita would listen occasionally, to check the competition. Arthur was invariably late; his theme music would be repeated until he showed up. And my wife reported with exasperation, "You get to work on time every morning—why can't he?"

NBC threw in every star it could muster against me, but it just couldn't make headway in the ratings. And our program director would panic with each new thrust. "NBC just put on Skitch Henderson! My God, how are we going to fight him?"

I had only one reply, "Never try to rewrite a hit."

An executive from NBC finally called me into a secret conference. "Do you know what our rating is in the morning," he muttered. "Zero!" Then he tried to lure me into coming over to NBC.

October 1949: WOR leaped into television—up to its ankles. All the other New York stations had started with a grand splash in the new medium: big-name movie stars, symphony orchestra, top stage and screen comedians, flashy production numbers, dancers, girls, girls. WOR didn't think we needed all that razzmatazz. In the interests of economy, I, as the dean of the announcing staff, was asked to open with a short welcome speech, to be followed by the studio orchestra with several acts the producer had rounded up around town.

Somebody wrote a speech for me, which I dutifully memorized. As soon as the little red light flashed on the camera, warning me I was "on"—I forgot the whole thing. I'd been ad-libbing for two decades, so I breezed along with my own introduction. It didn't matter—the sound went dead for six minutes. But nobody told me, and I just went on talking. Well, it was a night to remember. I was followed by a sort of vaudeville show of performers I'd never heard of, and comedy sketches with gags even more decrepit than mine. This went on for ninety minutes. I was persuaded to close the show by repeating my unheard introduction.

The reviews were murder. Harriet Van Horne wrote in the *New York World-Telegram:* "After twenty years of hearing John Gambling and not seeing him, WOR fans at last saw him and couldn't hear him. . . . WOR will be telecasting twenty hours a week from now on, but I can't help thinking they could have waited another five years." The headline over this read: WOR-TV PREMIERES IN A BLAZE OF SILENCE.

Variety reported: ". . . small-time programming added up to a virtually solid block of monotony."

November 1949: I went on, in my own weekly TV show, but what more could I say after my debut left me speechless? It was called *Get-Together With Gambling*, a cozy one-hour mishmash, with economy-size talent and audience participation. It was televised from the New Amsterdam roof theater on 42nd Street, where Florenz Ziegfeld produced his great intimate musicals of the twenties.

Before the opening, I was transformed into a kid of twenty by a Hollywood makeup artist. I was grotesque. I walked around the block, wondering if I shouldn't just say the hell with it and take a taxi home. But I steeled myself to go on. Of that debut, I can only recall a toothy Spanish soprano yodeling "When Irish Eyes Are Smiling."

Billboard magazine's critic said: "For the most part, the mike chitchat was of the non-irritant variety. However, the guileless gang of muscians should stick to their mutes and can the chatter."

My heart was not in it. In radio I was my own boss; I had my hand on the throttle all the time. Television was pandemonium. A very young director, whom I couldn't even see because he was hidden in a control booth, told me where to stand and when to turn. I felt naked, adrift in a leaky boat, with a map of the wrong ocean.

For visual fun, I brought back the singing canaries. I should have known that birds are more outrageous scene thieves than children. I picked up a birdseed sponsor, who demanded a commercial showing the bird eating seed out of my hand. All live, of course. But the bird wouldn't eat the seed. Their trainer discovered my feathered friend would eat it if mixed with finely chopped lettuce. The night of the show, as the sponsor beamed in the audience, the bird immediately pecked away at the mixture in my hand. The camera dollied in tight to reveal strips of lettuce dripping from its beak . . . and all the seed still in my hand. End of sponsor.

My favorite bird sat on my shoulder as I walked out to open the show. I called for a piano player in the audience,

and up came a pate smooth as a bowling ball. While he
played "Come Home, Bill Bailey," the canary tried to perch
on his head. It was so smooth the bird slipped off—but
it was stubborn, it kept on trying. The camera moved in
for a closeup as the bird dropped its opinion of the show,
right on the pianist's head. End of canaries.

After twenty-six weeks, I cut myself loose from TV. For
two good reasons: (1) I wasn't having any fun, and (2)
I wasn't making any money. If I had been doing one or
the other, I would have stayed on; the combination of the
two was just too much.

March 1950: My twenty-fifth anniversary show was
broadcast from the stage of the Longacre Theater, West
48th Street. Mayor Robert Wagner dropped in to say
hello. Bernarr Macfadden, chipper as ever at eighty-two,
stood on his head for the TV cameras. My father, eighty,
just as chipper, flew over from Cambridge for the party.
He forgave me for hocking that bicycle in Kilmarnock.
The ends of his waxed mustache jutted out like ibex
horns as he joined me and John A. in cutting the giant
birthday cake—the three Gamblings onstage for the first
time. (And last. Father died four years later.) John
Crosby, the caustic critic of the *Herald Tribune*, devoted
two columns to me that were rather affectionate despite
his cavils: "His voice is rather prim, quiet, a little stodgy,
and sounds faintly like that of an elderly Deems Taylor.
. . . Enormous changes have taken place in radio programs in Gambling's quarter century on the air, but he
remains persistently horse-and-buggy, as old-fashioned as
a cigar-store Indian."

Which may explain why I had become the long-run
phenomenon of radio. The audience loved the horse-and-
buggy, and wanted it to lead the parade. I didn't stand
still: I kept on making improvements. I began announcing the closings of schools due to weather, fire, epidemic,
coal shortages. I arranged with the schools for a secret
code so that some lazy senior with a deep voice could not
use me to escape a final exam. Occasionally, one did. And
once I closed down a school in New Jersey as the result of
a joke by one of our engineers. A letter from the principal

gave me a sharp slap on the wrist. Over the years, I made thousands of these announcements. The record was set in the winter of 1957, after a blizzard: On one day I shut down 1,030 schools. My reward? A hoarse throat for the rest of the day.

July 1952: *The John B. Gambling Club* made its so-so debut on WOR and the Mutual Network. Record music and chatter, 3:15 to 4 P.M., five days a week. The program director lured me into the show with: "There's a mint of money here, John. The network has 385 stations, and every one that puts on a local commercial during your show will pay you."

I said okay, if my son, John, could appear with me—to get experience and develop confidence. I had spent twenty-seven years building the morning show; it was now an institution and I wanted John to carry on. Some sons who stepped into their father's spots on radio made good—a lot did not. Al McCann's son did beautifully at WOR. The sons of Fulton Lewis and Lowell Thomas made it. H. V. Kaltenborn was anxious to have his son, Rolf, follow him, but the young man wasn't interested; he became a successful economist. Young John was willing. Was he able?

Variety liked the show: "It's all easy on the ear." It was also easy on the network's checkbook. In the six months it ran for Mutual, we never collected a penny from any station except WOR. Either the affiliated stations did not find a single sponsor—or they never reported it.

The show proved, I thought, that John could talk his way out from behind my shadow. WOR was unimpressed. Radio is a hard-nosed business. The men who control it measure success very simply: How much money do you bring in?

March 1955: My thirtieth anniversary show, from Madison Square Garden. The most thrilling day of my life. The station had 44,000 requests for seats; the auditorium accommodated 18,310. Lines started forming at the Garden by 5:30 A.M. in the eighteen-degree cold. Many journeyed from out-of-town. By 8:45, the auditorium was packed. The show ran for hours and among the

celebrants were Arthur Godfrey, H. V. Kaltenborn, Ed
Sullivan, and some of my neighbors from the Metropolitan Opera across the street: Lawrence Davidson, basso,
and Mia Slavenska, premiere ballerina. Young John was
master of ceremonies. Godfrey showed up late as usual,
at the Garden and then on his own show at CBS; but on
both occasions he recalled fond memories of our friendship and competition. After Mayor Robert Wagner appeared, Ed Sullivan quipped, "The mayor has finally legal-
ized Gambling in Madison Square Garden." Rita read a
poem for the occasion:

> . . . Thirty years have come and gone,
> Still John Gambling carries on. . . .

Thirty years! Still happily married, and doing well,
thank you. I had come a long way from the shaky day the
Limey sailor swallowed the anchor. I was indeed still
carrying on—harder than ever. I now carried three shows,
six days a week:

Rambling With Gambling, 6 to 7 A.M., Monday through
Saturday.

The Musical Clock, 7:15 to 9.

Gambling's Second Breakast, 9:15 to 9:30.

Still, WOR wanted to expand my time on the air. I was
fifty-eight years old. The moment finally arrived when I
told myself, John, it's time to retire. An engineer whom
I'd hired, back when I was in the engineering department
at WOR, had retired. Immediately, he and his wife bought
two plane tickets to visit their daughter in Holland. The
next day he dropped dead.

This hit me with an explosive jolt. I'd been negotiating
a new contract with WOR; the current one still had three
years to run. I had no intention of dropping dead the day
after I retired. I called my lawyer and told him to settle
the negotiations quickly—I wanted out.

Somehow, management did not believe me. They
thought I was being coy to raise the ante for the new contract.

They refused to let me out.

CHAPTER FIVE

GAMBLING WITH GAMBLING

My three-month-old son Noel
enjoys your program, and as
soon as you sign off, he falls
asleep.

Mrs. Brenda Z. Steere,
New York City

You certainly have an excep-
tional voice. I turn on your
show just to get the 8 o'clock
news; the minute you come on,
my baby starts screaming! The
only reason you got the job is,
your Father *owns* WOR.

Anonymous listener

I wish he had owned WOR—everything might have been so
much easier.

Was I good enough to follow my father? On this question,
management divided into two camps, just as in so many Euro-
pean wars of succession. I called them the Old-timers and the
New People. The Old-timers dated from before 1951, the year
when RKO General Inc., a subsidiary of General Tire and Rubber Co., bought the station from the R. H. Macy interests. The
New People came in with the change of ownership.

The Old-timers kept thinking of me as the four-year-old kid
who sang on his dad's show. They felt that my father should go
on as long as he could clutch a mike. Among the New People
who were willing to take a chance on me were Robert Smith,
the program director, and Robert Leder, at that time vice-president and general manager of WOR.

SMITH: The Old-timers said John couldn't make it. People
in sales felt he didn't have the voice, the personality.

Most people tend to be rather conservative when you start tampering with their bread and butter. Even Bob Leder had some nagging doubts:

> LEDER: I saw that John B. was building his son into his successor. I felt it could not work—yet. John A. was still green. I thought he would antagonize listeners into charges of nepotism. Did the audience really want him? . . . Nevertheless, some changes had to be made. I'd been brought in to increase the station's earnings. John B. generated a tremendous revenue—50 percent of WOR's gross. And because of his ironclad contract—he took a big percentage off the top, before discounts or agency commissions—he was reaching $500,000 a year. That was more than WOR's net. Now he was pushing sixty and, frankly, losing touch with the younger market. If we couldn't attract young people, the show would inevitably die. Young John was twenty-six. I decided to put him into a different kind of show, *Music From Studio X,* to give him training and develop him into a personality in his own right.

Bob Leder created the format and worked closely with me; Bob Smith helped me pick the music. The central concept was "easy listening"—lush music, high-fidelity—the music interrupted only every quarter-hour for weather, news, and commercials. It was frankly designed to counter the very successful nighttime programming of WPAT, Paterson, N.J.

WOR gave the show a lot of time and spent a lot of money in engineering and promoting. The schedule was cleared for 8:15 P.M. to 1 A.M., Monday through Saturday, and 1:30 to 5 P.M. Sunday. To make room for nearly thirty hours a week, nine shows were shifted. About $18,000 was spent to build a special hi-fi "Studio X." Each LP record was played only once, to reduce surface noise to a minimum. We also experimented with stereophonic sound. The broadcast was heard over WOR-AM and FM; if you had a set tuned to both frequencies, you received the stereo effect.

The music followed a middle path between "pop" and the classics: Percy Faith, Montovani, David Rose, Fred Waring, the Melechrino Strings, Broadway show tunes, plush vocals by

Jane Morgan, Jo Stafford, the Ray Charles Singers, and others. This kind of programming is commonplace today, but in 1956, it was considered "experimental."

The show opened July 9. Our first sponsor, Budweiser beer, came in two weeks later for a half-hour a week. Mutual Network affiliates lined up for the entire show or segments. We started with WIP, Philadelphia; WNAC, Boston, and affiliates in Dallas, Texas; Troy, N.Y.; Johnstown, N.Y.; and Wilkes-Barre, Pa.

Variety rated us "a pleasurable program, smartly tailored, building and sustaining a mood through the savvy selection of records. There should be a wide potential audience for this kind of programming."

There was. By the end of the first month, WOR's audience in that time slot jumped 17.6 percent over the previous month. The Pulse survey found that we had 885,000 listeners on an average night, in 508,000 homes. By November, our position in the New York market zoomed from fourth to first. *Studio X* ran four years and made management quite happy.

> LEDER: The show was very successful, and John matured as a broadcaster.

One problem: I hated the hours. I never enjoy working at night—I'm a morning person—and the show created a tortuous schedule, since I was doing the afternoon 3:15 to 4 show at the same time. Although I was young and bright-eyed and bushy-voiced, my family life started to fade out. The schedule wasn't quite as tight as it had been in Hanover, but the distances were greater and the hours longer.

I would leave our house in Munsey Park, Manhasset, at 1:30 in the afternoon, drive my old two-door Chevy into New York, and reach the studio about 2:30 for the 3:15 opener. Since this was smack in the middle of the daytime rush, there was always some doubt in the studio that I would make it on time.

> EVELYN VOLPE: It was five minutes after 3; John hadn't arrived yet. I was fidgeting in the office he shared with his father, wondering if this was the day John wouldn't make

it. With about four seconds to spare, he dashed in, tossed his car keys on my desk. "Get my car. It's in a no-parking zone!" And he ran to the door.

I called out, "Where?"

"Thirty-seventh and Madison!" came the voice from the hall.

It was during the height of the Christmas rush. But I found the car and as I tried to unlock it, this big, burly policeman came over to me.

"Is this your car?"

"No," I said. "It's my boss's."

"Is that so?" He was suspicious. "And who's your boss?"

"John Gambling."

He didn't believe that at all. "I hear him every day, and he doesn't sound like the kind of guy who'd park under a no-parking sign."

I murmured he'd been in a hurry, and I tried to start the car. Well, I'd just learned to drive—and I couldn't find the ignition.

The cop came over again. "Are you *sure* that's John Gambling's car?"

I muttered, "Of course." And just then, I got it started. The Chevy lurched to the middle of the intersection— and it stalled. The autos honked up a storm behind me, and the cop came over, fuming.

"Lady, you *sure* that's your car?"

"No, no. It's my boss's."

"You'd better get it out of here fast, or I'll have to tow you in."

The car started up again, luckily. And then it stopped. And started. I was never so embarrassed in my life. When I got it to 40th Street near Broadway, I pulled into a parking lot. It died immediately. I just tossed the keys to the attendant. "You take it," I said. "I've had it."

After the 4 P.M. signoff, I'd work in that office until 6. Then out again, for early dinner. I usually ate at Bleeck's, at that time a hangout for newspaper people, in the old *Herald Tribune* building on 40th Street. I had a table in the corner and I would eat while I read a book; that's where I got into the habit of reading thirty-five to forty books a year.

At 7:30 I'd walk back over to 1440 Broadway, where I was locked in from 8:15 to 1. I'd drive home and arrive at 2. And so to bed. Friday night (really Saturday morning by the time *Studio X* ended) I stayed in a hotel in the city, because on Saturday morning I subbed on the *Rambling* show for my father, starting at 6 A.M. Then I'd drive back to Munsey Park that morning and drive back to New York at 6 P.M. for *Studio X*. Occasionally, I'd vary the routine by taking the train home for dinner after 4 o'clock, the train back to the city for *Studio X*, and drive home again after 1 A.M.

> SALLY: We certainly didn't see much of John. Fortunately, Ann and John R. came home from school for lunch. John would get up at about 11:30 and have his brunch with our lunch. About 1 o'clock he'd drive off, and the children didn't see him again till next day's lunch. They had to go to bed after *Howdy Doody*.

The pace began to grind me down. One night, driving into town, I fell asleep in the Queens Midtown Tunnel. No accident, but some scare. WOR now agreed to let me pretape the Saturday night show.

A worse shock hit me a few months later, one that made me fear I'd reached the end of my brief but hectic career. Each night I grew progressively more *hoarse*—I could barely talk by the end of the week. I asked a neighborhood doctor for a remedy; he gave me a lozenge and sprays. No help.

I tried a second doctor, who was reputed to be very successful with the vocal maladies of opera singers. No help.

I was about to sit down and write my resignation to Bob Leder when a friend suggested a New York throat specialist. He took one look and announced, "You've got a polyp on your vocal cord."

Polyp? Was this cancer?

"It's the equivalent of a wart. Could have been caused by a bruise when you were very young." He sent me to the clinic at Temple University in Philadelphia, where Dr. Chevalier Jackson specialized in removal of polyps. It was only a half-hour operation but it put me out of commission for two weeks. I recuperated on my aunt's farm on the Eastern Shore of Maryland; talk was forbidden, and I could only communicate with Sally by writing little notes. For two weeks, I was off the air. And off cigarettes.

The hoarseness went away. Several weeks later, the tensions of the two shows got to me, and I resumed smoking. I've always been an optimist. My basic attitude is: It'll turn out all right. Too bad that polyp happened, but everything is going to turn out. And for a long time I had no trouble with my throat.

Suddenly, about three years ago, my voice turned hoarse again. I started hacking and coughing. I rushed back to the doctor who'd rescued me before. He rigged up a mirror so I could look down my own throat and see my vocal cords.

"What color are they?" he demanded.

"Pink."

"They're supposed to be white, milky white. They're pink because you talk a lot and you smoke too much. Furthermore, you have some small spots—these could be latently cancerous. If you can stop smoking, your cords will turn white again in two weeks and those spots will go away."

That was it. As I walked out of the office, I reinforced my basic optimism with a massive dose of willpower: I threw away the cigarettes and haven't touched one since. And, yes, my vocal cords turned milky white.

In any event, they were good enough on *Studio X* to convince Bob Leder that he wouldn't lose much by gambling on me. Some of the sales people still urged him to keep Dad on with me: Let the kid do the show, but we want John B. to do the commercials. My father and I and Bob rejected that notion. Dad did agree to fill in for me when I went on vacation, to help ease the transition.

By early 1959, everyone was on the same wavelength about the future show; only the question of money needed to be finetuned. *Only?* Obviously, I could not expect to be paid what my father was earning after his thirty-four years on WOR. I would have to work for considerably less, even though I would have to work considerably longer because *Rambling With Gambling* was to be expanded in length and scope. Well, I welcomed that.

Eventually, Bob Leder, with a lot of faith and good humor and firm belief in the divine right of management, put the whole package together. I received an eighteen-month contract for about $100,000 a year, plus a percentage of the revenue. That's what the newspapers reported. What they didn't say was that the contract could be canceled by WOR, after thirteen weeks, if they were unhappy with me.

> LEDER: This was three or four times the money that John was worth at the time, but he had qualities that would make him a success. . . . The most difficult job in the late fifties and sixties was finding powerful performers with believability. This was a very strong quality in his father. People had grown up with John B.; he was an old friend, a neighbor, an old shoe that fit well. We believed that John had this quality, too.

I started *Rambling* solo on October 5, 1959. There was no big brass fanfare of welcome, and no hail-and-farewell ceremony. My father and I had been working on the show together for about a year; on October 5 he simply was not there. That's the way he wanted it. I was twenty-nine and, sure, I was nervous; Dad exuded strength and confidence just by being in the studio. I felt very much the same as the night I'd awakened in my car in the middle of the Queens Tunnel: I was surprised to be there, exhilarated at being alive, and I had to keep going.

The format remained, for a while, very much the mixture as before. Changes crept in gradually, ever so slowly. The radio audience was changing; the buying and selling of radio time changed with it. Let George Brown, vice-president in charge of programs and news, explain the technicalities:

> BROWN: When I came here in 1945, morning radio was not an important source of revenue. Those were the days of network radio, very similar to television today. The nighttime periods, which were network time, were the big moneymakers. Daytime was second, and morning was third. Morning time was sold in quarter-hour segments. The sponsor paid for fifteen minutes of time and the talent to fill it. This was very expensive, and only large companies could afford it.
> In the fifties and sixties, there was a tremendous expansion of automobile owners, and people driving to work in the morning and returning early in the evening. The

advertisers call these periods "drive time." This greatly increased the value of morning shows that catered to the needs of motorists. Bob Leder came in as general manager in 1956, as these changes occurred. He found that commercials could be sold in one-minute spots, or less. Also, these spots could be rotated; one day they appeared at 5:45, another day at 9. This created more revenue and more advertisers.

The running time of *Rambling* was expanded. The 6 A.M. start was moved back to 5:30 and eventually to 5. *Breakfast With Dorothy and Dick* was moved ahead an hour, so that I picked up the 8:15 to 9 segment. Peter Lind Hayes and Mary Healy, who succeeded Dorothy and Dick, left WOR a few years ago, and the program expanded again to 10 o'clock. All this gave us more time for public service and entertainment.

The music went through a major metamorphosis. My father had a predilection for Strauss, Lehar, and Sousa—music to exercise by. This was not my taste, and I didn't think it appealed to many listeners my age. I carefully filtered in some of the music that had been so successful on *Studio X:* Broadway show tunes, Kostelanetz, Frank Chacksfield. After a while, these faded into what I judged to be the best of contemporary music. Not hard rock. In the fifties and sixties, most other daytime shows flipped for rock 'n' roll, country and western, rhythm and blues, everything loud, louder, LOUDEST. I felt our show should gentle the people out of bed and off to work. Nobody wants to be jarred out of his shorts in the morning.

WOR has an expert in the science of demographics, Howard Selgar. He spends his days collecting and analyzing statistics of the shows: size and composition (age, sex, economic levels) and geographic distribution. He told me a large part of our new audience was young people, in the 25 to 35 age group, which was indeed fortunate for the future of our show. They probably had been rock fans when they started listening to radio, at the age of five or so. They'd grown up with it; it was as natural as breathing and eating corn flakes. But now, they were tired or bored with it. They swung over to our show. The sound was young enough, and so was my view of life.

Over 95 percent of Dad's audience stayed with me. I still get letters from the traditionalists asking, rather plaintively, "Why don't you play the lovely melodies your father played?" What can I reply? We're in the seventies, not the thirties, and I am not, after all, my father.

The arrival of that omniscient philosopher and gentleman wit, Peter Roberts, expanded our news coverage and opened new vistas. Just as my father had done for years, I delivered the five-minute half-hourly news summaries. Although I did an adequate job, delivering the news is a specialty and I couldn't do it as well as a man who made it his life's work. Bob Smith, who'd known Peter at WINS, suggested that here was a newscaster with a plus—a sense of humor.

Peter had also sparred verbal rounds for two years there on the Bob (Elliott) and Ray (Goulding) show. He had a quirky sense of humor and so did I. If we came together, we might send off a few sparks. As soon as Peter moved over from WINS in 1962, Bob told me, "After the newscast, pick up a light item and kick it around."

> ROBERTS: I met John for the first time on a Friday afternoon—we were to start together on Monday morning. I'd never heard the program before; I usually worked late on my other jobs, and got up late. . . . We agreed at the first meeting that nothing would be written down, so we'd be free to experiment. Since I didn't know John, I didn't know what his responses would be. I felt the only way to work it out was to just let it all come out on the air. So, on Monday I came in at 6:30, read my five minutes of news, and then we started right in to ad-lib one of the items. It was pretty funny.

It was kismet, predestination, or dumb luck. Neither of us is a comedian; no funny voice or a mad, upside-down vision of the world. But his gently quizzical tone contrasted with my quick verbal jabs. Although the old comedy pros of radio, stage, and TV have an axiom—you can't make a comedy team out of two straight men—we bent that a little.

When Peter and I go out on personal appearances, many

people ask, almost apprehensively, "Those funny things aren't written out, are they?"

I assure them we are totally unrehearsed. They sigh, relieved: "Oh, that's good."

One of us, usually Peter, will come in with the skeleton of an idea, based on a news item or whatever is lurking in the back of his ever-mysterious mind, and we take off from there. It could consist of likely candidates for the Secaucus Grand Prix, or Peter's laundry list, or the John Gambling Research Foundation's study of the mating ritual of the American grackle. We toss these ideas back and forth twenty-four times a week, which is a lot of funny material to ad-lib. Of course, some of it isn't funny. It just goes *splatt*. But even Jack Benny and Fred Allen didn't unbuckle the bellylaughs on every line. We enjoy it, and that sense of sudden fun communicates itself to our audience. Except for the loner who keeps writing, "Bring back Rosco and Frosini!"

We developed better techniques for scouting traffic flow from the air and extended that coverage. Before 1962, our information came from a small single-wing plane. And it was chancy.

> BROWN: Bob Schmidt piloted that plane, and he had to fly at 2,500 feet because of federal regulations. One year, the plane was unable to fly 40 percent of the time because of adverse weather. It was an expensive and unreliable operation.

Helicopters had been used in Los Angeles and Chicago; we were the first in New York. As Fearless Fred Feldman flew up, up in Helicopter 710, audience loyalties went up, up with him. There seemed to be a double benefit in his reports. You could use his warnings of traffic tieups to get to work on time—or as alibis to sleep late.

Dr. Bob Harris came in two years ago to help expand our weather-forecasting center into the most complete private system in this area. He built a network of volunteer observers who loyally call in weather conditions from all over the tri-state area. Our forecasts are the result of Bob's hour-by-hour analysis of weather conditions, and so they are more meaningful locally, I'm convinced, than the federal government's National Weather Service.

Don Criqui made us champs in sports with a coverage we'd never had. Jack Allen joined us about six years ago to round out our news team with Harry Hennessy and Henry Gladstone, both of whom had been delivering the hourly fifteen minutes of news when fifteen minutes was considered an eon.

Dad filled in during my vacation for three years, then bowed out. "I want to retire all the way," he insisted.

> JOHN B: From the day I retired, I felt a great big stone had rolled off my back. No more lunches with advertising agencies and sponsors. No more looking up at that clock, no more split-second schedule, no more squeezing in all the commercials. . . . A lot of people don't believe that anybody in the public eye can be happy out of it. Marie Torre, who was radio-TV editor for the *New York Herald Tribune*, called me in Palm Beach when she was doing a series on retired people. She wanted some retirees from radio, and she couldn't find any. They were all hanging on. I said, "I'm no authority on retiring as yet, but I'm very happy about it." She wouldn't believe it. About three months later, she met Evelyn Volpe, who was my secretary and then John's, and Marie asked her, "Tell me confidentially, is Mr. Gambling *really* happy?" It's hard for people in New York to imagine that anybody can be happy leaving New York.

To illustrate how unobtrusive our changeover was: Many listeners, when they meet me, will murmur, "My goodness, I expected you to be a much older man." I explain that I am actually a remarkably well-preserved seventy-five, due to clean living.

Confusion over our names compounded the confusion. In the year before I soloed, my father and I worked together on the show. Dad always referred to himself as John B.—a touch of the English formality. When we signed off, he would say, "This is John B. Gambling" . . . and I would say, "This is John A. Gambling, wishing you a good morning." Then when he retired, I kept using my middle initial out of habit. In a little while, I realized that made me sound too formal; I dropped the middle initial.

In the minds of hundreds of thousands in our audience, the continuity of *Rambling With Gambling* has remained unbroken since 1925. Many think my voice and my father's are identical. The reason: They have never heard us together. Our voices have a certain family resemblance, but our thirty-year difference in age creates a difference. Dad in his prime, was deeper, more resonant. Since the pace of the show is much tighter today, my tone tends to be crisper.

From the very beginning of my succession, listener reaction was overwhelmingly positive. If it hadn't been, WOR had its escape clause. The letters we received generally followed this theme:

"When your father retired, I felt nobody could ever replace him. We listened to him so long, he was part of the family. But you've done a grand job and we still listen to you."

Some letters proclaimed, "You'll never be as good as your old man."

But in the light of my personal philosophy, things have turned out rather well. The *Rambling With Gambling* audience is the largest of any single radio show in the United States: We accumulate over two million listeners in an average week. By contrast, my father's show drew about one million. The advertising revenue from his show peaked at $2 million; ours has doubled that. There's only one statistic I've never been able to top Dad in—his early bedtime.

Years ago, Mother explained his feat in a little poem she read on the Christmas show:

> How does he do it, you all say,
> How does he get up before break of day?
>
> . . . Just remember while you had a date,
> John Gambling went to bed at 8!

I rarely get to bed before 9. Which brings me to what is virtually the Number One question from listeners:

"What time do you get up in the morning?"

CHAPTER SIX

EARLY TO BEDLAM

I have a way guaranteed to keep
you from falling back to sleep
after your alarm goes off. I
sleep all day and work most of
the night, so I could phone you.
Then call back in fifteen minutes to make sure you're up. I
have a very pleasant voice—
some men say it's sexy—so getting out of bed would be a
pleasure. I'll even call you "Darling!" What's more, I won't even
charge you a cent.

(Miss) Diane Churchill
Queens, N.Y.

The inevitable next question is:

"*How* do you get up in the morning?"

The inevitable answer is:

"Slowly, and with two alarm clocks."

3:15. My Distant Early Warning goes off. It's a hand-wound
Big Ben alarm that sits on my dresser, about ten feet from the
bed. That alarm forces me to get out of bed—to shut it off.
But I don't let any clock bully me; I crawl right back into bed.

3:30. The electric alarm, shrill and insistent. That's it. I roll
out and decide it's another day.

In twelve years of tight-schedule sleeping, I've snoozed
through, or miss-set, that second alarm about a dozen times.
Sometimes by more than half an hour. But when that "inner
alarm clock" we all possess finally does wake me up, it's with a
terrible jolt, followed by that sinking feeling in my stomach:
My God, I've overslept! I've let everybody down . . . guilty,

guilty . . . Then I tell myself that everybody else is late once in a while, why not me? I call the studio to assure them I haven't been canceled in an accident. And they assure me it's okay, and Peter Roberts is standing by to fill in. By that time, Sally is awake because I'm making so much noise, thrashing around to put myself together quickly. Guilty again.

3:32. But on a typical day I amble downstairs into the kitchen for what passes for breakfast. I don't eat a good old cereal-ham-eggs-toast-jam-coffee meal recommended by nutritionists to start the day right. I just eat whatever's handy. I don't think it's fair to ask Sally to get up to cook, so I've become the world's most skillful refrigerator raider. I'm a picker and a sampler. If there's some juice or fruit in there, fine. If there's a cold lamb chop left over from dinner, I'll snatch that, too. Or vegetables. Or a peanut-butter sandwich. Or some cold crab claws. My, they're good at 3:32 A.M.

The *spécialité de maison* that I need to get me started at that hour is strong, hot tea. That really pops my eyelids open. And I'm a great water-boiler. I turn on the radio while boiling to catch the news, thoughtfully provided by a competitor. This fills me in on what's happened since I went to sleep.

Moving faster now, I climb the stairs again, carrying the tea with me. The grandfather clock in the hall chimes the quarter-hour. Its *bing-bong-bong* is a pleasant memory from childhood; the clock graced all the homes of my parents until they moved to Florida.

3:45. Shower, shave, and dress. Roughly in that order. It's been some time since I dressed before I showered. But it has happened at that hour.

Basically, I'm a pretty conservative dresser. I like good clothes and have my suits and sport jackets and an occasional pair of slacks made to order, but a half-dozen suits are adequate. What I wear to work depends on (1) the weather and (2) what I have to do after the program. During the winter months, I struggle into a coat and tie almost every morning. Unless it's one of the Fridays when we're going off skiing. Then I can usually be spotted in a turtleneck shirt and sweater.

In the summer, it's a different story. Unless I've got a luncheon date or a business meeting in the city, a sport shirt, slacks, and jacket are the uniform of the morning. After all, whom do you see that you want to impress at 5 A.M.?

Most of the men in the studio dress informally, too, and we all work in shirtsleeves. Except the newscasters. I don't know what it is about newscasters, but they are a formal breed. Blue business suits, dark ties, all conservatively cut. And they always wear their jackets when broadcasting. Strange.

Oh, yes—my one minor fetish. I wear only striped neckties. Why? I *like* striped ties. Sally buys them for me, and happily she likes striped ties, too.

4:18. Finally ready to go. Sally accuses me of being the world's slowest dresser. On weekends, when we are preparing for a sortie into the normal social world, Sally is almost always the first dressed and waiting. The reverse of the standard joke. Maybe because I am confined to such a rigid, structured schedule for five weekdays, when Saturday and Sunday come, I like to wander even more as I dress. I listen to the radio, stare out the window, examine my closet for moths. But we're usually the first to arrive at the cocktail party. Punctuality is a habit I can't lick.

4:20. The Carey car and driver are waiting, and we're off to New York. I drove back and forth to the city every day for years and really didn't mind it. But as the show got longer, and I got a little older, I found myself growing very drowsy as I drove home around noon.

I'm in the studio by 5 at the latest. There is about fifteen minutes leeway here for me. The show actually opens with my recorded voice—"Good morning. It's Wednesday. Welcome to *Rambling With Gambling.* Now here's Jack Allen with fifteen minutes of news." At 5:15 we go into music, then I come on live at about 5:18.

Sometimes I'm hardly alive. These are the times when Sally and I go out on a weekday evening and get home pretty late, and I've had one more drink than I thought I had. I still have to get up at 3:15. Thanks to the old adrenalin that kicks up when the "on-the-air" lights come on, I've managed to struggle through the program with a hangover and only a couple of hours' sleep. If any listener can identify one of these mornings—don't tell me.

And sometimes I run into snow and storm. When a storm starts dumping snow in the afternoon—and Dr. Bob Harris tells me it will be a mean one—I just don't go home. I hole up in a hotel. But I have never yet been prevented from reaching the studio by bad weather. My secret: getting up at 3:15.

Most tieups in rough weather are not caused by the snow itself but by drivers who don't know how to handle snow. They don't have proper tires or chains, or brains, and they become the "abandoned vehicle" that ties up traffic on a major road. At the dim hour I travel, very few drivers are out, and these guys are the morning regulars; they know the roads and the tricks of getting through. A road can be safely open at 4 A.M. and turn into a nightmare of ice, snow, and stalled cars an hour later.

One time I was late, and I can't blame it on oversleeping, or the weather, or a lost driver. It was the morning our youngest, Sarah Jane, was born. Sally had been examined by the obstetrician just the preceding afternoon, and in his infinite wisdom he had assured her the baby was due in two or three weeks. It was a miscalculation that I rank with the British charge at Balaklava.

Sally, with pains, woke me at about 2 A.M. I called the doctor and after some discussion about "time and intensity," he admitted, "I guess you'd better go to the hospital right away. I'll meet you there."

Sally demurred, with her woman's prerogative. "I want to take a shower first, get dressed, pack my bag, and so on. When I'm ready, I'll go to the hospital."

I fell in with the casual mood. I figured I might as well get dressed, too, and ready for work. You never know about babies. We finally made it to the hospital by 4:15. The doctor was anxiously waiting and took Sally right into the delivery room. I sat down to wait, at least for a little while. The show at that time started at 6, so I thought I would have to leave the hospital no later than 5:30. But when I put my finger on the button of the elevator, outside the delivery room, the doctor came out to announce, "Your daughter has arrived."

I took time to see that both Sally and Sarah were just fine, and then happily hit all the green lights between Manhasset and 1440 Broadway. (Well, by that time all the lights looked green.) I was in the studio only one minute after 6—late, breathless, but very pleased to announce the newest addition to the family.

On the days after Sarah Jane was born, and before Sally brought her home, I would get up half an hour earlier than usual and stop in at the hospital to see if all was well. The nurses in the maternity wing seemed to welcome a visitor at what was probably the low point of their night—3:30 A.M. They would have coffee ready for me, let me see Sarah and talk to Sally if she was awake. And one morning, they even let me take pictures of Sarah Jane. She couldn't have been more than three or four days old. You see, there is some serendipity in getting up at 3:15. And I hoped the morning audience enjoyed my daily hospital bulletins on Sarah Jane's progress.

4:12. My driver has picked up a paper on the way out, so I read the *Daily News* during the drive to town. It gives me another point of view on what's broken out in the world since the sun set. I'm looking for news and features while reading for my own pleasure. I have to know what stories the papers are emphasizing that morning.

Have you ever noticed that people read a paper by habit? What I mean is, they read certain parts of the paper in the same order every morning. I do. I start with a quick glance at the front and back pages of the *News*, then check what the stock market did the day before, and then I turn to the pictures in the centerfold. If either the editorial or the feature story catches my eye, I read it next. And then I go back to the front and start a thorough page-by-page reading, front to back. And I almost never vary that routine.

Unless, of course, I've put a couple of dollars on a horse the afternoon before. I will, on occasion, use my Off-Track

Betting phone account to play a hunch or two. Five bucks to win is my top, and usually I'm a loser. But hope springs eternal, and so a quick look at the results from The Big A or Bowie changes my reading pattern.

4:55. Car pulls up in front of 1440 Broadway. I hurry down the marble-lined corridor, wait for the elevator. Bill McEvilly, my producer, breezes in. Very natty in white knit shirt with red stripe, red-and-blue-plaid knit pants, tasseled mocassins. He's really a rather conservative guy, but today he's hoping to play golf after the show.

"How was your golf lesson?" he asks.

"I'm hitting it a ton. Next week, the tour."

5:00. Jack Allen is on with the news in Studio 5. Studio 2, my studio, is about 15 by 20 feet. Sea-green carpet, alternate stripes of acoustical cork and beige vinyl on the walls.

I sit facing the control room, at a large table shaped like a horseshoe, what Peter Roberts refers to as the "famed Studio 2 U-shaped desk." I have two microphones, both suspended on booms. I use the one facing the control room for the greater part of the show. The other, to my left, I use when I'm chatting with Peter, Don Criqui, or one of the other newsmen. They sit at a rectangular table along the left wall. The natural tendency is to look at the person with whom you're talking, so the second microphone is used to keep me from wandering off mike Number One.

Directly in front of me on the desk is a unit we call the "iron man." This is a bunch of buttons, a small microphone, and two dials. I use this to communicate with Bill McEvilly and the engineer in the control room, to select what I'm hearing in the hearing-aid type of earphone I wear while on the air, and to control the volume of the music in the studio and in the earphone.

My commercials and announcements are on reading boards, or racks, on either side of the iron man. I have an alphabetical accordion folder handy, in which other commercial copy is filed, and a triple-decker letter bin sits just to my left for filing news I've used, weather, transit bulletins, commercials, and even jokes. We save everything I use on the air. I never know what some listener is going to write and ask about weeks after the broadcast. Rule Number One—save it!

By 6 o'clock, when I'm well into the show, the desk is covered with papers, news clippings, coffee cups, and music cartridges. All the music and the recorded commercials are played in the control room, but the music is filed in this studio, so I can pick and choose in a hurry.

The iron man also has a "cough button." Rarely do you hear anyone cough, sneeze, or wheeze on radio, thanks to this button. When the frogs act up—and they will do that especially in the morning—a quick jab at the little button cuts off the mike for a precious moment to clear the throat.

I'm surrounded by clocks. Two in the studio and one in the control room. Everybody working in Studio 2 has a clear view of at least one clock. These units are connected to the Naval Observatory in Washington. Their hourly time *beep* is automatic, and they never vary by even a fraction of a second, correcting themselves electronically. I also have a digital clock on the desk, giving me the day and date. It's a handy reminder; nothing sounds more stupid to a listener than announcing the wrong date.

5:02. Bob Harris brings in the morning weather map and latest reports. "This fair-weather system will last only a day," he warns.

"I have a golf date this weekend, Bob. You'll have to do better than that."

5:05. Bill McEvilly and I sit down to check the commercial schedule. I work from a rundown prepared the day before by my office. Bill has an IBM printout, WOR's master log, of all commercials: their length (10, 30, or 60 seconds) and whether they're live or recorded.

McEvilly: ". . . Buick Opel, 30 seconds, ETA-2 . . ." (Shorthand for: The sponsor is Buick, it's recorded, it's 30 seconds long, and the correct tape cartridge is number A-2.) "Leisure Village, live . . . Texaco, ETP-1 . . . Di-Gel—"

JAG: "Let's move the Di-Gel later, between 7:15 and 7:30."

McEvilly: "Canada Dry . . . Alpo pet food . . . Aqua Velva . . ."

On an average morning, the schedule will call for about seventy commercials between 5:15 and 10. The Federal Communications Commission recommends that there be no more than eighteen minutes of commercials in each hour of broadcasting, and WOR strictly adheres to this limit. About half of our commercials are live. I try to space all of them as evenly as possible through the show. And I do my best to keep them palatable and pleasing.

5:15. Music: Carole King—"Sweet Seasons"

5:18. This is where I come in, live:

> *Good morning, a hearty welcome to you on this fine Wednesday morning. Join us on* Rambling With Gambling, *and all the crew is here—Peter Roberts, Fred Feldman, Harry Hennessy, Don Criqui. It's a clear, bright day, and the trains and subways are all running on time, and here's the weather. . . .*

And we're into the day. I may make some last-minute changes in the sequence of commercials or public-service announcements, but the show is set and rolling. I know people may wonder, perhaps with some irritation, how I can be so cheerful so early in the morning. The truth is—I can't help it; I am naturally optimistic. Sure, some days I would rather have stayed in bed. But I know the listeners aren't very happy about getting out of bed, either. They don't want to hear my problems. One of us has to be cheerful.

I have a theory about the early morning. For the average family, it is probably the worst time of the day. It is a time of tension, of train and bus schedules to meet, children to get dressed in clothes they usually don't want to wear, water that takes forever to boil, bacon that overcrisps, and too many people trying to get into too few bathrooms.

I firmly believe that the last thing listeners want to hear, in this controlled mayhem, is more noise, more confusion, more controversy. There's enough of that right in their own kitchens. So *Rambling* has always tried to make some sense out of a bad time of day as pleasantly, as sanely, and yes, as quietly as pos-

sible. Leave the shouters and screamers and arguers for later.
5:30. My news spot:

> *There is no strike on the Long Island Railroad—yet. The*
> *strike scheduled for today has been postponed while nego-*
> *tiations continue. . . .*

While reading, I signal the engineer to pick up some musical
numbers I want to use after the news. All of our music is on
tape in cartridges, something like the 8-track tapes played at
home or in the car. Except there is just one number on each
cartridge. I like to feel my way with the music, to fit the
mood of the moment, the weather, the day of the week.

Hundreds of 45 rpm records and LPs are produced every
month and they flood into WOR's record library. John Mc-
Carthy, head of that department, auditions and rejects about
60 to 70 percent, stuff he knows I won't play. Most of them
are just too noisy, too rocky, too long, or just plain stupid.
What's left, he brings down to the studio, and we listen to
them and talk them over. And then I toss out 50 percent of
those. What's left I play on the air.

When I think a song is "right" for the show, I'll stick with
it. Unlike the formula radio stations that play only the "Top
40" hits of one week, I'll repeat songs that were popular a
year or two back—my "Golden Oldies." How do I know
what's "right"? I guess it's some sort of sixth sense I've developed in twenty-two years of selecting music. Only one record,
which doesn't fit the pattern of the show, may cause a listener
to tune out. That's why I've always picked all the music for
the program.

> *. . . and a warrant has been issued for a former New York*
> *City policeman, accused of masterminding a $150,000 rob-*
> *bery in the Municipal Building. . . . In the Sudan, Premier*
> *Gaafar al-Nimeiry has warned the opposition . . . .*

I read the 5:30 news "cold"—without a previous scan. I
just don't have the time for it. Our WOR news writers are

clear thinkers and knowledgeable, so it should read well. How do I know the pronunciation of complicated proper names? There's nothing to it. I just charge ahead . . . with absolute authority. Most people believe broadcasters always pronounce words correctly. So, right or wrong, we're way ahead. The problem is to remember how you pronounced it the last time.

Music: Percy Faith—"Wives and Lovers"

I have full control of the running order of the show. Sometimes I have to change the sequence of music or a commercial. A two-way talk-back system connects me with the control room. But, obviously, I can't be talking to the audience and telling the engineer to switch commercials at the same time. So we resort to what Cro-Magnon man used thousands of years ago before he learned to talk—hand signals.

I use my left hand to signal commercials and the right for music and promos. If I want an airline commercial to come up, I flap my left hand like a bird's wing. For a soft drink, beer, or coffee ad, I pantomime drinking out of a cup. For a bank, I pull out my wallet. The left hand, pointing, means a one-minute ad; crossed fingers, a half-minute; looped fingers, that's all, end it. Pointing with the right hand brings in music; one finger held up, a promo; a fist means the WOR musical jingle.

The trick here is to do one thing while saying another. It's no more difficult than scratching your head while you pat your stomach. I've also developed the ability to read one thing and think another. I will occasionally find myself, in the middle of reading news, thinking of my golf game or a business lunch. It can be disconcerting.

5:58. Jack Allen hurries in for his 6 o'clock report. He loosens his tie and rolls up his sleeves to his elbows. Jack happens to be the only newscaster who doesn't work with his jacket on. He marks pauses and corrections with a black pencil and . . .

6:00. "Here's Jack Allen with the news."

The normal routine of Studio 2 is, on occasion, disrupted by the wide world outside. The space and moon shoots are a good example.

If an American can get to a convenient TV set, chances are he'll watch the launching or landing rather than bend an ear just for the description. But there are thousands and thousands of people in cars, at work, or in those nooks and crannies where the tube can't be found. So, as Jack Allen, our space expert, sits in with me, we cover space travel from a TV set in the studio. We pick up and rebroadcast the voice of Mission Control and the astronauts, and intersperse our own comments. A bit more primitive than the Apollo landing system, but it is effective radio reporting.

One morning recently, Jack and I had our eyes glued to that TV screen, earphones clamped on to monitor Mission Control, our mikes open, and all systems go. The glass between our control room and the studio reflects enough for me to see what is going on behind my U-shaped desk. As Jack and I continued our reporting, I noticed that the back door of the studio was opening. A very tall man in some kind of uniform entered, followed by a much shorter man in a business suit. I followed their reflections as they walked over, stood behind my desk, and watched the moment of blastoff on TV. After the rocket was safely on its way, the short man nodded with satisfaction and the two walked out the same quiet way they had come in.

Since we were on the air, not a word had been exchanged. Much later, I was told I had been visited by the Governor of New Jersey, Bill Cahill, and his bodyguard, a formidable New Jersey state trooper. The Governor was appearing on the Martha Deane show that morning.

And I didn't even say hello.

6:30. Peter Roberts is on with his news. He wears his jacket —always. I walk out. This is no criticism of Peter's work. It's just that I've been sitting in that high-back, black vinyl swivel chair for an hour and a half. I need a stretch . . . and I want to make sure the sun has really risen today. So I walk into the newsroom and look out the window.

CHAPTER SEVEN

"YOU CAN'T USE FRIED POTATOES IN A POKER GAME"

Today you said you can't shoot a camel in Arizona, but you didn't explain *why*. This law was passed when the U.S. Army imported a group of camels from the Near East in the 1850s. They were sent to Arizona, just before the Civil War. With the war on, this experiment was abandoned and the camels left to carrying freight for the Army across the Arizona desert. After the war, some of these camels escaped or were let loose to run wild in the desert. They continued to breed in the wild, and as late as the 1940s there were unconfirmed reports that a camel was seen in the desert. See: Report of the Sec. of War in Respect to the Purchase of Camels for the Purpose of Military Transportation. Washington, 1857.

Jacques Noel Jacobsen, Jr.
Staten Island, N.Y.

The sun has come up . . . sort of. Under the soupy haze I make out a tower that could be the Empire State Building. So I guess everything is all right. I come back to the studio for a public-service announcement:

. . . the 1972 world championship horseshoe-pitching tournament, Saturday through Monday, at Mountainview Park . . . the best tossers in the world.

Music: The Carpenters—"Superstar"

During this, Bill McEvilly brings in a transit bulletin, and we start yakking about golf. Bill is embarrassingly good—he carded a first in the Wykagyl Bowl tourney last year—and he asks about my pro's technique of teaching with mental images.

"He wants me to imagine the swing," I explain, "as if it starts at my right hip pocket and ends up with my right hand following the motion of skipping a stone over water. With the club ending up high over my left shoulder."

"And where's that little ball you're supposed to keep your eye on?"

"In the sandtrap."

Music: Engelbert Humperdinck—"Everybody's Talking"

For no reason the thought hits me: How many thousands of hours have I talked, and how many millions of words, how many commercials, in twenty-two years of broadcasting?

> *. . . here is the cylinder lock that no intruder can pick open. And now it's combined with an alarm system that sounds off if any attempt is made to jimmy your door or window.*

7:15. Fearless Fred Feldman from Helicopter 710:

> *. . . we have a car going southbound in the right lane of the FDR Drive. The hood is up and the driver is under it, looking for trouble. So be prepared to squeeze to your left and look for extensive delays on the FDR.*

And you can be sure that in about two seconds the driver will pull his head out, slam down the hood, and buzz off. And a string of motorists on the FDR Drive, who don't have to squeeze, will think Fred is faking it, or blind. Or both.

Music: The Vogues—"My Special Angel"

7:30. Peter Roberts and the news. He's beautiful. He still has his jacket on to complete the ensemble—banker's dark blue suit, light blue shirt, black-framed glasses.

7:45. And here's Don Criqui with the latest sport news.

Music: Roger Williams—"Gentle on My Mind"

I do a bit off the news wires:

> *At Brighton, England, an eight-inch earthworm, named Tom-Tom, captured a worm race at the International Toy Fair today. Tom slithered across a two-foot glass course in a record-setting one minute, seven seconds. This is a speed of two-hundredths of a mile per hour. Tom's owner, a toy company executive, said "Tom was trained by the Chessington Zoo and fed a secret diet." . . . I wonder if worms like fish as much as fish like worms?*

8:30. Peter Roberts again, and still in his jacket—although he does take it off when he's writing in the newsroom. Strange. After five minutes of news and a quick weather check:

> *. . . a report from Picayune, Mississippi. A skunk crawled under the living room of Mrs. Dorcas Duncan here. It was startled by the sound on the TV set of a rocket being launched at Cape Kennedy. The animal immediately fired its own retro rockets.*

Picayune, Mississippi? Impossible. Often I'm afraid we can't tell the difference between what we improvise and what is reality. Dr. Bob Harris, in the control room, is laughing along. (Peter later showed me a U.S. atlas—there *is* a Picayune. A small point.) Now a commercial:

> *How do you think your dog feels when he bites into cereal instead of the meat he's accustomed to?*

Music: Frank Sinatra—"The Girl From Ipanema"

9:00. The maintenance man for the clammy air-conditioning arrives while Harry Hennessy is on the air from Studio 5.

JAG: "It's terribly humid in here."

MAN: "It's humid outside, too."

JAG: "If it snows outside, does it mean we have snow in here?"
MAN (seriously): "There's no window in this room. How could you have snow?" Exit maintenance man, satisfied he's done his best.

9:15. The Woman's Auxiliary of the Spofford, Connecticut Volunteer Fireman's Association is having a luncheon and cake sale....

I try to deliver twelve or fifteen public-service announcements every day. They arrive in my mail by the thousands, so I divide them up geographically and include a variety of events. They are an important dimension of the show. I could announce all the big-time glamour benefits and galas and dinners, but they receive plenty of publicity. The smaller church bazaars don't. I'm just as happy talking about events that may involve a hundred people or less in a small town in New Jersey or Long Island. They keep the program on a local scale, in the largest urban concentration in the country.

9:20. Bill brings in a bulletin he's taken over the phone, detailing the Transit Authority's latest breakdown. As I read it, he holds up a large map of the subway system and points to the stations affected.

The New York subway system is a mess. And as a result, reporting delays is not one of our great services. Until a few years ago, our coverage was spotty at best. The TA dispatchers were often "too busy" to answer a radio station's phone calls requesting information. Don't call us—we'll call you. And many minutes passed before we found out about major tie-ups. Bill McEvilly persevered and was able to establish a rapport with a number of TA morning dispatchers. Finally, at the urging of other stations, a "hot line" system was set up to transmit transit information to all radio and TV stations in the city.

I still receive letters every week, usually signed IRATE SUBWAY RIDER, blaming me for not reporting long delays the previous morning on the IND "E" trains. But until some Orwellian time, when we can actually monitor subway operations from a big lighted route board right in the studio, we'll just have to depend on the TA for our information. Condition: better, but not great.

9:30. It's Peter Roberts again. And, yes, he's still got his jacket on. Five minutes of news, and he has a hot report from Kennedy Airport. They've expanded again, with new seats and more space to accommodate more people waiting for more seats on more planes.

> JAG: *That will only create a bigger traffic jam. Did you ever try to get to Kennedy on a Friday afternoon in a car?*
> ROBERTS: *Did you ever try to get to Kennedy on a Friday afternoon in a plane?*
> JAG: *It's a big mistake. They ought to rip out the new seats, wall up the new space, to make* less *room. That way they'll have* fewer *people coming in to Kennedy. That's how to solve the problem.*
> ROBERTS: (after more news): *U.S. airmen stationed in England have been ordered by their commanding officer to cut down on their weight. He said, "Give up your weekly trips for those fish and chips—"*
> JAG: *The chipskate! Do you know what fish they use with chips? Fried cod.*
> ROBERTS: *Oh, no, no. They have a flat European fish called plaice—P-l-a-i-c-e.*
> JAG: *If it was my place, I'd use ordinary cod. I always say, be it ever so humble, there's no home like plaice.*
> ROBERTS: *And they use French-fried potatoes for the chips.*
> JAG: *That's ridiculous. You can't use fried potatoes in a poker game. The cards get very greasy. That's what drives the deuces wild!*
> ROBERTS: *I pass. Now here's a story from Hong Kong. Three French gastronomes finished a 72-course Chinese imperial banquet. And you know what one of these experts called the greatest delicacy, mild and fresh? Bear paws.*
> JAG: *Bear paws?*
> ROBERTS: *Of course. It's the pause that refreshes.*
> JAG: *This all happened in Germany?*

ROBERTS (restraining himself): *No, no! Hong Kong! What gave you the idea it happened in Germany?*
JAG: *Germany has the Black Forest. That's where the legendary gastro-gnomes live!*

9:45. For the telephone interview, I have a young lady, Bobbie Stevenson, who tried out recently with the San Antonio, Texas, All-Stars semipro baseball team. These interviews are set up by Bill McEvilly a day or two ahead. I like to do them live rather than on tape, so you have the immediacy of the moment.

Radio discovered the telephone only about five years ago. Phones had been used sparingly in direct coverage for a number of years, but always with an annoying *beep-beep* in the background. The FCC felt the *beep* was needed to make it clear that the conversation was being broadcast. This requirement was finally dropped, and suddenly the telephone became the most useful radio news tool after the microphone. There are telephones where even our mobile units can't go.

I have discovered a rather amazing fact as I interview people each morning over the phone. If they had to come into the studio and sit in front of an impersonal, threatening mike, I suspect they would be nervous and even reluctant to talk. But over the phone, speaking from the familiar surroundings of their home or office, my guests are relaxed, articulate, and fascinating. Ma Bell is a great helpmate.

In fact, I think radio today has only scratched the surface of techniques in which the phone can be used in news coverage, entertainment, and community service. Years ago, the Hooper radio-rating service would call to ask what station you were listening to. Tomorrow, WOR may call—and you'll be on the air.

Here's Bobbie Stevenson:

JAG: *Did you get a job with the All-Stars team?*
BOBBIE: *No. I choked up on the bat, and the manager choked up when he saw I was a girl.*
JAG: *Did you really expect to make it?*

BOBBIE: *Sure. I've been playing for a couple of years on a men's softball team, and I'm second in runs batted in.*
JAG: *Do you get a separate dressing room?*
BOBBIE: *We don't have dressing rooms. We change in the car.*
JAG: *What about showers?*
BOBBIE: *Oh, they just sap your energy.*

Music: The Nashville Brass—"Walking the Floor Over You"

9:59.50. . . . the latest news at ten, with Henry Gladstone, then Martha Deane and her guest at 10:15. We'll get everybody back together bright and early tomorrow morning for more Rambling With Gambling *right here at WOR Radio, New York. Have a good day. It's 10 o'clock."*

*

And that's it. It's been a morning like many other mornings. We haven't changed the world, but we've helped a million people grab a toehold on a new day.

It takes about fifteen minutes now to clear my desk. The news, weather, and commercials are filed away. I call my office in Long Island to see if all is well there. And to tell my secretary what time I would like the going-home car to pick me up.

I stretch and walk around a little. I've been at that U-shaped desk for five hours, with only three short breaks. And I've got one more hour of taping to do.

I may relax with a cup of bouillon. Our kitchen is a walk-in closet at the rear of Studio 2, with its little refrigerator and hot plate. A glass pot of water is constantly bubbling. The kitchen is stocked with coffee, tea, cream, instant soups, sugar, juice, crackers, and yogurt. The last is for McEvilly. Bill does the ordering, I do the paying, and everybody does the eating and drinking.

I get back to the desk about 10:20 to tape the Saturday show. I originally did the Saturday program live. About seven years ago, the six-a-week schedule began to weigh me down. WOR relented. Now I tape my talk part of the show, commercials, and the intros to the music and repartee with Peter. After I'm finished, at about 11, Bill puts it all together on tape. On Saturday, these taped segments are integrated with the live news and weather.

We don't make any secret of the fact that the Saturday program is part tape and part live. In fact, the FCC insists you cannot even imply that a program is all live when a part of it is recorded.

On tape, I can still give frequent time signals, usually accurate within a few seconds. Listeners are often curious just how it's done. Easy. Many years ago, when I first started working with my father, we prerecorded an afternoon show for the Mutual Network so that Dad could get home and sleep. In those days, before tape, the recording was done on large acetate disks. And there was no way to edit out the mistakes as you can with tape today. Since timing for the network had to be even more accurate than the way we operate today, we needed some sort of accurate timing device. I started with the most expensive, complex clocks, timers, and stopwatches in town, but each had some flaw.

And then, miracle of miracles, I happened on a photographer's darkroom timer, made by Kodak. It's bright red, about the size of a large alarm clock, with adjustable minute and second hands, and an on-off switch. Perfect and accurate. And cheap. I must have paid $5 for the first one. In the twenty-odd years we've used this beauty, Kodak hasn't changed the design one bit. We've worn out three of them, and the only change is—the last one cost $12.95.

Now, here's the secret of those simple, accurate time checks. I know from the cartridge labels how long each musical selection runs, as well as the length of each recorded commercial. I set my timer, say, 7:15, and start talking. I introduce a commercial, stop the tape, and move the clock ahead one minute. I start the tape and clock again, introduce a song, stop the tape, and move the timer ahead for the number of minutes and seconds the song will play on Saturday. Presto! When I start the tape and timer again, the timer gives me the exact minute I've reached on the tape and on the air when Saturday comes.

One trick. I just can't look at the real time on the real clock on the real wall. I've got to keep my mind fixed on that great come-and-get-it day . . . next Saturday morning.

After taping, I have perhaps one luncheon and two or three business meetings a week. Otherwise, I start for home by noon. The car and driver are waiting, and now I have forty-five minutes all to myself in an air-conditioned, cushioned cocoon. I use it happily. Some days I dictate answers to listeners' letters or business mail on a small tape recorder. I dictated most of this book in the car, so if the print jiggles before your eyes it's due to the Long Island Expressway's rough paving.

Or I read. I like a good mystery by Helen MacInnes or Agatha Christie. Or *The Day of the Jackal*—what an insidious thriller! I'm something of a Civil War buff: I have a good library on that war at home. I can become absorbed in almost any novel set in the past—C. P. Snow, Mary Renault, Morris West —and I never pass up a good sea story. When I'm into a book, I'll pick it up again with a cocktail, before dinner, and then drop into it for an hour or so before I go to sleep. I read about a book a week.

The car pulls into the driveway of my house a little over an hour after we leave New York. It takes me almost twice as long to get home around noon as it does to come to work in the early morning. Usually, I bypass much lunch because I try desperately to keep my weight down. But since I'm already in the kitchen to look over our personal mail, I poke into the refrigerator for a quick inventory . . . a slice of melon, or a plate of shrimp, or yesterday's hamburger. Sally comes in to say hello, and I pick through the leftovers as we talk over plans for the rest of the day, what's new with the children, and what she's done this morning.

Before heading in for my nap, I go to the offices we've built in the house, to check with Evelyn and Marie Peterson, her assistant, and make a phone call or two. I try to make all my business calls in New York before I leave for home. If I call from Plandome after 12, everybody is out to lunch; you can't reach any businessman in New York, even to tell him his office is on fire, between noon and 2. By 2, I'm usually lost in my nap —and you can't tell me my office is on fire.

I'm on my feet again by 4, refreshed and reasonably ready for anything. After a cup of tea and a chat with Sally, if she's home, I'm back upstairs for a couple more hours of office work. Answering letters, sorting out the requests for personal appearances, declining invitations to back Broadway shows and, of course, signing checks.

I am an incorporated business, John A. Gambling Enterprises, Inc., and must cope with all the vexing day-to-day problems faced by any small businessman. Sally, the corporation secretary, is an important part of my business team.

A while ago, the *Wall Street Journal* ran a thorough article about *Rambling With Gambling*, in which it called me "King of the Morning Men." Being a business-oriented newspaper (and one of the three I read each day), the story paid special attention to the commercial aspects of the program. How much money WOR makes from the broadcasts, the costs involved in putting together a program like this, and finally, how much money I make.

The article stated that I was the highest-paid radio broadcaster in the nation, with an annual salary of $300,000. That's a lot of money, and I must say the figure is reasonably accurate. I say "reasonably" because my annual income depends on many month-to-month variables. Such as the price sponsors pay for the commercials, the number of spots in the program, the length of the commercials, etc. And the overhead. WOR provides all of the equipment and pays all the people who work with me at the studio. My corporation employs my secretaries, extra production help, my substitute when I am on vacation or sick, and pays for any business activity away from the studio. I do not "own" the program. *Rambling With Gambling* is a WOR property for which I am hired, through John A. Gambling Enterprises. It sounds a bit complicated, but it's worked rather well for a lot of years.

By 5:30 or 6, I'm downstairs again for one or two cocktails. We sit down to dinner at about 7:30, and I'm usually in bed by 9:30. In the summer I'll work extra hard to keep one afternoon open for golf. On these impetuous days I rush out to the club by 12:30, have a quick lunch with three friends, who also sneak off for an afternoon, and play eighteen holes. For this, I am willing to forego my nap. Although it usually means an earlier night to bed.

I guess, when you get down to it, no day is ever typical. And that's true of everyone's life. What makes this job of mine constantly exciting and challenging is: When that red light goes on at 5:15, there is just no way of knowing exactly what will happen in the next five hours. The President has been assassinated, the city has blacked out, men have walked on the moon and returned, and the railroads and subways still run late. We're there to cover the big stories and the little one, the best way we know how.

When I say "we," I mean Our Gang.

CHAPTER EIGHT

INSIDE THE SECAUCUS GRAND PRIX: PEACHES FLAMBÉE EXPOSED

> ... Your courteous treatment of Dr. Bob Harris and the others assisting at WOR is refreshing after the wisecracks so many of the "star" performers make. Please keep it that way.
>
> > John F. Cuff, Jr.
> > Danbury, Conn.

> I'm sure that Dr. Bob is a wonderful person, but perhaps he should enter some other line of work. The only time he's right is when it's impossible to be wrong. Grandpa's seagoing eye and Grandma's corn are better prognosticators.
>
> > Ernest F. Thompson,
> > Yonkers, N.Y.

You hear eight people in addition to me: Jack Allen, news; Peter Roberts, news and staff wit; Don Criqui, sports; Dr. Bob Harris, weather; Fred Feldman or George Meade, helicopter traffic reports; Harry Hennessy and Henry Gladstone, news.

The personalities and lives of these eight men have helped shape the show. And sometimes the show has molded their lives. Most of them don't live in the public eye—radio, unlike television, gives its people anonymity. You may recognize their voices off the show, but their faces—rarely.

Yet these voices represent only a fraction of the team needed to put the show on the air. These are the WOR people whose voices you never hear:

Bill McEvilly, our producer.

Mario Sfogliano and Matt Bayliss, the engineers who take turns operating the controls in Studio 2, on-air or recording, from 5 to 11 A.M. Two more engineers are on duty in other studios to handle newscasts, special events, and remotes.

Jim Yoell, who has overall responsibility for operation of the WOR newsroom. His three writers prepare some of the newscasts; several of our reporters write their own.

There are more engineers at the Linden, N.J., transmitter and the FM transmitter at the Empire State Building, where the communications center for our helicopter is located.

And then you must include the men and women in the program and sales promotion and maintenance departments. I figure thirty-two people contribute to our show. That's what makes it seem so easy.

The engineer is the first man in the studio, at 4:45 A.M. He checks all the cartridges for correct running order. I have selected the music the day before, and the night production manager has brought in the recorded commercials.

John Cook, our engineer who retired last year, probably heard more Gambling shows than anyone in the world. He started with my father in 1935. In the time scale of radio, that's the equivalent of going back to the Roman emperor Augustus. Every morning, I'd see Cookie through the glass panel of the control room, alert, smiling, enjoying each moment, and on his feet. That's right—he stood for five hours. And he was sixty-eight.

> COOK: I had to stand so I could move fast to the recording and cartridge equipment. They're set up so I didn't take my eyes off John. I wore nonskid rubber soles. [The engineers who replaced him sit.]
>
> When I started, the pace was slower. The show was shorter and a lot simpler. We had time to break up John B.—but he never did. He was a perfectionist, and more intense than his son. John B. knew exactly what he wanted and you had to do it exactly his way. He and I got along beautifully all those years because I'd been a ship's

radio operator, too. And, funny coincidence, this job at WOR was my first one off a ship, just like his.

I miss Cookie. I'm sure he's just as cheerful and fast on his feet in his garden in Elizabeth, N.J., as he was in our control room.

Bill McEvilly sits about ten feet from the engineer in the control room. As producer, he is my right hand—and my left. He makes certain everything is right where I need it—ads, news, weather. Bill knows how to laugh, but usually he looks dour, as if he sniffs rubber burning in a cable. Most important, he's in a constant state of unflappability, solid as the granite on which 1440 Broadway sits.

MCEVILLY: I was brought into production when the show started at 7 A.M. and John B. would come up from Palm Beach to fill in during John A.'s vacation. His father was irritated by the time we spent on the helicopter reports. Fred Feldman would be on for a minute and a half, and John B. would mutter, "He's too long, I'm going to clip [cut] him!"

John A. had to make changes. He carried over for a while his father's custom of announcing golden weddings and birthdays of people eighty and ninety years old. Trouble was, John would announce the ninety-first birthday of some dear old lady in Wappingers Falls, and next day I'd get a call from relatives that she'd passed away.

The transition from his father's Strauss waltzes came quickly. When Frank Sinatra was romancing Mia Farrow, he anchored his yacht and Mia in the Hudson at the 79th St. marina. Fred Feldman, on his traffic tour downriver, spotted the ship early in the morning. John dreamed up a romantic situation in which Fred was to say, "I see a dark, slim man looking over the rail at the sunrise," and pretend to lower a mike to the yacht. And then we would fade in, over the roar of the helicopter, a Sinatra solo. The trouble was, I couldn't find a single current Sinatra record! Luckily, Martin Block's record library was down the hall; I ran out and borrowed a Sinatra from him. So our audience heard Frank singing "It Was a Very Good Year." By the end of that year, we'd run a lot of Sinatra—and we were out of Strauss.

During the morning, I communicate with Fred or

George in the helicopter, and keep in touch by phone with
the Transit Authority, police, and railroads.

John thinks and talks instantaneously; it's a talent he's
honed fine in many years of broadcasting. The newscast
he reads at 5:30, for example, is brought in from the
newsroom just a couple of minutes before. Since he
reads it cold, he has to scan ahead of what he is saying on
the mike to spot typos and correct them. Without stop-
ping.

His father was even more adept. He would *write* a note
to Johnny Cook, selecting the next piece of music, at the
same time he was reading a commercial.

You'd be surprised at the amount of humor around
here so early in the morning. There is no temperament,
and John's attitude breeds cooperation. He doesn't criti-
cize; he understands when people make mistakes.

I owe a great deal to Jack Allen: my ability to breathe easily
at 5 A.M. That's when I'm due in the studio, although I don't
always make it, and that's when Jack is always there with the
news, to cover for me. Jack is our expert on space shots and
politics. He has anchored the Republican and Democratic con-
ventions for WOR; a hardworking, supremely competent re-
porter and newsman. And a very solid citizen: close-knit family,
children in college, wife active in politics in Metuchen, N.J. He
just doesn't fit the role that Peter Roberts and I have created for
him—a martyr to martinis (or the "crystal yumyums"). Listeners have heard us reveal the graphic details of Jack's martyr-
dom: how he fell into the pool at the Metuchen Country Club
while playing Santa Claus . . . how he danced all night on tables
with a hat made of a Tiffany lampshade. We're only kidding, of
course. Otherwise, how could he operate the WOR Mobile
Unit, speeding through the dark of morning?

> ALLEN: And what's more, I have custody of that baby. I
> leave home in New Jersey at 2:30 A.M. and drive the unit
> into the city. It's a Chevy with two-way transmitter, AM-
> FM, and police radio. The station calls me if it has a job
> for me on the way in. After my 6 o'clock newscast, I shift
> to Transit in the newsroom. I phone every railroad in

town for operation reports. When there is a subway breakdown, I call McEvilly on our hotline, and he checks out the details.

At 9 A.M. I go out on the road with the Mobile Unit. If something big breaks, I can come in on John's show for a two-way report. I alternate with Lester Smith on the space shots, live from Florida. I did all of them, starting with John Glenn, until I left the Mutual Network in 1965.

I broke into radio in New Jersey in 1947. And for the benefit of any fans who collect useless information, my full name is Jack Allen Potts.

Peter Roberts has become an important asset to the program. I look forward to our exchanges as much as anyone in the audience. They're a challenge.

Several years after my father retired, he decided he didn't want to continue subbing for me on vacation, since it meant coming up from Florida in the cold of winter and the heat of summer. Both WOR and I agreed the best and logical substitute for me would be Peter. Three years ago, when I gave up the Sunday show, he took over in the morning time slot with a show called, peculiarly, *Rambling With Roberts.*

ROBERTS: I crept into radio in a rather roundabout way. From Canada. I started in college with the idea of becoming a lawyer, but I never finished. I came down with tuberculosis and spent four years at Saranac Lake, N.Y. My doctor advised against going on with law because it would weaken me. Somehow, I thought radio would be an easy kind of life; I walked into a station in Saranac, and they took me on for a couple months. I've been working long hours ever since.

On my dialogues with John: Judging from the letters we receive, people seem to welcome our analyses of the trivial and irrelevant as a change from all the scare news every day. Yet we manage to get in our satirical digs at some important problems.

To dramatize our satire, we've invented a group of characters who have become more real every day:

Camille Glockenspiel, the famous harpsichordist. Always in concert.

Mavis Winesap, Chicago debutante whose mother was a McIntosh.

Fawn Beige, the colorful ecdysiast.

The towering lovely, *Ponderosa Pine.*

Dame Maude Plankton, noted oceanographer.

Izzata Kimono, Japanese designer.

Peaches Flambée, our sex symbol, who first appeared in the Secaucus Grand Prix in 1967. The Grand Prix is, of course, the third most important road race in America. It's renowned for the first-time entry of the French four-cylinder Porte Cochere.

Sometimes I think John and I are visionaries. The wild fantasies we invent often turn into realities. We thought it was far-fetched when we dreamed up the Secaucus Grand Prix, with a racetrack on the shores of the "beautiful Hackensack River"—one of the most polluted bodies of water you can smell. The Rotary Club actually was happy we were putting the town on the map. And now, a huge sports complex is going to be built there to house the New York Giants football team. Plus a Disneyland-type park and, yes—a racetrack.

Then there was the John Gambling Research Foundation, "a nonprofit organization," which we invented as a device for awarding preposterous prizes. Well, our listeners began to write for answers to genuine problems, and solutions to do-it-yourself projects, and we had to go into some real research to reply.

I received a package in the mail from a printer in White Plains. He had printed up some stationery, with a solid, handsome letterhead on bond paper, listing the officers of the Foundation. For free. We use it for official business, and I've bought all my other stationery from him.

ROBERTS: I think one reason our repartee has been successful is, we're not close socially when we're off the air. We do get together about two or three times a year, but my wife and I have a different way of life. John has a typical family with three children; we have none. The Gamblings live on Long Island; we live in Upper Montclair, N.J. This gives us variety and perspective in our viewpoints. So we can still surprise ourselves on the show.

There was a certain tenseness in John when we started.

After all, he'd stepped into something big and he had to produce. His sense of humor has increased enormously and his reaction to life is a little more tongue-in-cheek.

Don Criqui is one of the most knowledgeable—and certainly best-looking—sports broadcasters in the country. He's even acted in a movie with Charlton Heston. Don is another one of us who got a start in college radio: After Notre Dame, he became an assistant to Frank Gifford at CBS-TV, and has kept one foot in radio and one in TV ever since. It's a good thing he's only thirty-one, because if he has to broadcast a football game on the West Coast for TV, he takes the notorious "Red-Eye Special" plane from L.A. that evening and jets into New York early in the morning, with just enough time to rush over to WOR to prepare his sportscast for our show at 5:50 A.M. Still, he looks so tanned and healthy, I sometimes think he leaves his TV makeup on.

> CRIQUI: No, that's really me. Especially the red eyes. Now, about that movie: Some of my best friends, including my wife, didn't call it acting. It was really me, playing a sports reporter. The picture was *Number One,* in which Heston played an aging quarterback, and it was a real loser from the kickoff. The New Orleans Saints provided the football background; I knew the manager and he suggested me for the part. I had all of fifteen lines. That generated a few phone calls from producers later, but nothing came of them.
> I still do the college and pro basketball for CBS-TV, and an afternoon show for Mutual, heard outside New York. My four shots on the Gambling show appear at ten minutes to the hour. I write the reports myself, from the wire services and from my own sources. Of course, if some producer wants to make a movie or a family-type TV series about a young sportswriter who commutes between the two coasts, and has a lovely wife and four photogenic children, I just happen to have a lot of inside stories. . . .

Now to Bob Harris and the weather. He's been with us about two years, a native New Yorker who has a Ph.D. in geophysics.

I call him Doctor Bob, first of all because he's entitled to it and, secondly, to convey the image of a kindly old Mr. Chips, peering over our weather machinery and bringing in his carefully reasoned judgments. Bob is, of course, anything but in his dotage.

Some of the guys in the studio used to call him Doctor Flipper —they claimed he flipped a coin for his major forecasts—but I can assure you, they're just being flippant. When the weather doublecrosses Bob, he feels as if he's personally betrayed a million listeners. It hurts him physically, spoils his entire weekend.

> HARRIS: We do manage to achieve 85 to 90 percent accuracy. Weather-forecasting is a science, but not an exact science. Occasionally we add two and two and get five; another time, we'll get four.
>
> Since I came here to head the WOR Weather Center, we've expanded facilities until now we undoubtedly have the most fully equipped weather center for broadcasting in the entire metropolitan area. Dr. Vincent Cardone, assistant professor of meteorology at NYU, works here on Sundays and when I'm on vacation. The two of us turn out all of WOR's forecasts, broadcast between 5 A.M. and 5 P.M.
>
> The center has three teleprinter lines: weather from every airport in the U.S.; a direct line to all National Weather Service offices in the East; and one from Washington that brings in soundings from the upper atmosphere. Our own radarscope shows all the active weather within 250 nautical miles of New York City. Two facsimile printing machines bring in weather facts and maps from all over the world. We have installed instruments on our roof at 1440 to give the latest wind speed and directions, dew point, rain, and snowfall.
>
> The machines are backed up by our volunteer observer network. About forty-five people cover an area of fifty miles in every direction from the city. They phone me, collect, starting at 5:45 A.M. and continuing to 9 A.M. with "naked eyeball" observations—the amount of fog . . . are the streets icy? . . . what streams and rivers are flowing over their banks. An enormous range of people work with us: a nun in the Maryknoll headquarters at Ossining; a retired Navy captain in Eatontown, N.J.; a faculty member of Stony Brook College, Long Island. About a third

are housewives who have their own rain gauges and thermometers. So John can say, "Right now in Maplewood, N.J., it is snowing heavily, the streets have two inches of snow." No other radio station in the city can do that.

I come into the studio about 3:15 and prepare the first forecast, given by Jack Allen at 5. I also prepare a weather map of the Continental United States and the Caribbean for John. He is quite erudite on weather, and he is able to interpret it very well. It requires a well-organized mind, because a tremendous volume of data is constantly being fed to John through the entire five hours.

People wonder why we can't be 100 percent accurate. Well, weather is a combination of rapidly changing factors; it is a question of timing. We know whether the weather will be good or bad; the "when" is the problem. Before the Memorial Day weekend of 1971, I proudly announced on the air, "I am so happy that I can promise all our listeners a lovely weekend." It turned into one of our most memorable rainy weekends. On Monday I received a telegram from a gentleman named A. Boyle, which I framed and hung on our Weather Center wall: PROMISES! PROMISES!

Despite all our electronic weather gear, we still rely heavily on the reports of people—our own, as they drive to work. Henry Gladstone comes in from Long Island, as I do. Bill McEvilly and Harry Hennessy drive in from the Bronx. Our New Jersey contingent comprises Bob Harris from Hillside in Bergen County, Peter Roberts from Montclair, Essex County, and Jack Allen from Metuchen, in Middlesex County. So we get a wide-ranging, down-to-earth view of road conditions in four or five key areas.

For the view of the man higher up, like 1,000 feet, we have Fearless Freddie Feldman.

CHAPTER NINE

HAVING A BABY 1,000 FT. OVER THE VAN WYCK EXPESSWAY

> There is one thing that has puzzled me, and that is the weather report. I often hear you speak of "ground fog." What I would like to know is: How in the world do they grind it?
>
> Carl F. Schmid
> Dover, Del.

Major Feldman (he's in the Air Force Reserve), with his lean, square-cut jaw and tightly gripped pipe, struck me as Fearless Fred as soon as he came on our show. And my nickname has stuck with him ever since.

He is also Friendly Fred. Since he is the only bachelor in our aggregation, he has time to play tennis, and he used to fly with me on my odd hours. Several years ago, he dropped in on the family to wish us a Merry Christmas. He landed Helicopter 710 right on the snow crust of our back yard. The children were delighted. This was the modern, electronically rigged Santa, with whirly-blades instead of reindeer. And instead of the conventional red fur-trimmed costume, Fred wore his workclothes. He refused a glass of holiday cheer (he never imbibes while flying), but we did persuade him to stay for Christmas dinner. He sat down at the table in his good old high-visibility orange flying suit.

FELDMAN: I've always wanted to fly, ever since the age of eight. I remember picking up a book about the Air Force titled *AAF*, and that settled my fate. My full name is Alfred Armin Feldman—A.A.F.! At the start of the Korean conflict, I entered the University of Connecticut,

majoring in philosophy and sociology. I guess I wanted to
be a friendly, thinking pilot. I finally made it to flight
school in 1954 and came out eager to be a hot pilot in
F-86 jets. But I'd picked up some problem in my ears as
a kid, swimming and diving, so the AAF put A.A.F. in
something less demanding—helicopters. I served in Korea
and Japan with the air rescue squadron; back in the
states, I ended up as a jet instructor. I opted out of the
service, and I bounced around with a couple of commercial helicopter firms.

Keystone Helicopters got the contract to fly for WOR
in 1962—and picked me, since I was a native New
Yorker. Two weeks before I was to start flying, I learned I
was expected to broadcast, too. The other traffic operations in the U.S. had two men in the copter, and the only
talking I'd ever done on the air was to control towers.

Well, we had to develop a whole new electronic system
so that I could use both hands to fly the machine. We still
use this Mickey Mouse headset: two mikes (one to talk to
the control tower and the other to WOR) and three radios
so I can hear the tower, WOR, and our production desk
(Bill McEvilly) for the cues. It was more confusing than
Korea, but it worked. I became the first man in America
to combine pilot and broadcaster.

I owe John a lot for helping me in the beginning, and
being a big enough person not to worry about building me
up. That's a terrific trait in him—he doesn't worry about
his position.

In 1963 the station decided it would be better to buy
its own helicopter. Even alternating morning and evening
with George Meade, it's a dangerous operation. Depending
on the weather, we fly at from 50 to 2,000 feet; in the last
dozen years a dozen weather pilots have been killed in
the U.S. But you have to live with it and outwit it and not
sweat it.

I had a close shave a few years ago. I'd taken off from
LaGuardia Marine Terminal with visibility dropping
rapidly. By the time I got to the George Washington
Bridge, I could hardly see my hand on the controls. And
then I realized I was under the Triboro Bridge. It was
winter, and the only thing that saved me from going into
the river was the reflection of the bridge lights on the
water.

I spotted two lamp posts in the fog—they were on Ward's Island, under the bridge. I landed all right, between the lamp posts. I was shaking in my boots, and the studio immediately asked me to give a foot-by-foot description of my descent in the fog. Then the police came, out of nowhere, and wanted to give me a ticket for illegal landing.

While I'm making my seven broadcasts in the morning, I have to concentrate on five or six different operations at the same time—flying an inherently unstable machine, watching air traffic and cars on the ground, looking out for jet blasts and winds, or rain or snow, scribbling notes for my reports on a clipboard, and broadcasting. Occasionally, I pour myself a cup of water or light my pipe. When I finish my last report, about 8:40, I'm a very tired lad.

I'm a bachelor, not because of philosophic choice, but because I haven't found the girl who's nutty enough to put up with me and the job and those hours.

When Fred's not flying, he spends considerable time speaking to schoolchildren. He gives lectures, with slides he has taken over New York, on pollution and traffic problems. He also has a series of slides on the people of Korea; through a foster-parent plan, he helps support an orphaned Korean child.

Fred is really concerned about the world outside the copter; he worries about those drivers in the strangled traffic. He is just as concerned as Bob Harris is about an unfulfilled weather forecast. That may be part of the key to their success—and the show's. We care.

Our other helicopter pilot, alternating with Fred every month between our show and John Wingate's in the afternoon, is George Meade. He's George only on WOR. To his family and friends he is always Binky. He explains that his father, who was nicknamed Bucky, tagged him with Binky the day he was born. But WOR management didn't think Binky sounded substantial enough for a helicopter pilot. Too much like a character in *Winnie-the-Pooh*. So I dubbed him Jolly George, or Gorgeous George, or Uncle George.

MEADE: Anyhow, under the name of Binky, I flew 1,000 combat missions in Vietnam (1966–67). In UH-1B ("Huey") choppers for combat assaults, supply, and medical evacuations. After I came out in May, 1968, I couldn't find a job in commercial aviation—or any kind of aviation. By that time I was twenty-five. I needed a job in order to get married. I signed up as a sales trainee for a medical supply manufacturer—and the day before I was to start, I got a call from Butler Aviation. One of their men was out sick and could I come in right away?

I flew all sorts of missions for Butler: copter taxi for U Thant and Sidney Poitier, also filming *Hello, Dolly!* and the Alpo pet food commercial, and I worked for CBS Radio's traffic reports. I'll never forget my first minute on the air. I announced, "I'm over the George Washington Bridge and—" That was all. I froze up for thirty seconds. Nothing came out.

Eventually, I recovered, and I worked the CBS afternoon show for several months. In April 1969, I came over to WOR and worked afternoons, filling in on John's show when Fred went on vacation. We began to alternate our jobs in October 1971.

When I work the morning show, I'm keyed up all the time. It's a big audience of constant listeners and, I think, more attentive than the afternoon audience. John is a demanding person to work with, but he makes me feel that when I'm on—"You've got it—go ahead. Don't worry about John Gambling—you're the star right now."

Like the time I was having a baby 1,000 feet over the Van Wyck Expressway. I'd rushed my wife to the hospital at five minutes to 6, dropped my two-year-old daughter, Tracy, at her grandmother's, rushed out to LaGuardia and taken off for my traffic report.

I called in from the copter to Bill McEvilly: "I gave the doctor your number in case he wants to get in touch with me." I gave my report at 7:09 A.M. At 7:18, Bill said, "I don't know when you're on next. Just monitor the station." And I hear John talking about my wife, soon to have a baby, and I thought, gee whiz, I didn't expect him to announce this all over three states.

Suddenly, John says, "We just got a call from your doctor, George, and you are now the father of a girl."

First I thought he was kidding, and my next reaction

was right in line with Phase II of the President's economy plan: "John, think of all the dimes you just saved me!"

A couple of days later, when I came home, the doorstep was covered with cards and letters, and gifts of knitted bootees and scarves for Colleen. Talk about a responsive audience!

Harry Hennessy, who's on with fifteen minutes of news at seven and nine, also came out of college radio—Cornell. He was drafted into the army, narrated training films for the Signal Corps, later joined WOR as summer temporary in 1946. In the early fifties he broadcast the 7 A.M. news as part of my father's show.

> HENNESSY: John B. had an instant sense of humor. The engineers went on strike once, and the staff had to make its way to the old transmitter in Carteret, N.J., to get on the air. Dorothy Kilgallen and Dick Kollmar did their show from their own home; this day they couldn't make it to Carteret. So John B. and I had to fill in their forty-five minute spot. John announced, "We normally have the Dorothy and Dick show now, but they're not here this morning. Harry, would you rather be Dorothy—or Dick?"
>
> My broadcasts now come out of Studio 5, on the twenty-fourth floor. I wake up a little before 5 A.M. and switch on the radio to catch Jack Allen. If any big news has developed, I'll come into the studio earlier. Usually I reach the studio about 6:20.
>
> These hours have a great advantage—I can go home in the afternoon to enjoy our two adopted daughters. We adopted the first, Caroline, here in New York when she was an infant. The other, Maryanne, is thirteen now. She's half-Korean, half-American, and we found her through an agency that specializes in placing foreign war orphans. It has been a fascinating experience; my wife and I have learned so much from her.

Several of our newscasters have become specialists in an area of their own. Harry, who is Catholic, has done a great deal of research in the history of the Church. He was sent to Rome to cover the election of the last two Popes, John and Paul, and for the sessions of the Ecumenical Council. Henry Gladstone has, ever since the U.N. moved to its quarters in New York, interested himself in the people and workings of that organization and covers important events there for us. And Jack Allen is our expert on space shots.

Henry Gladstone is a neighbor of ours on Long Island—he lives in Roslyn—and a close friend. He's an enthusiastic sailor and long-distance yacht racer. In fact, Sally and I have chartered his boat, a 38-foot Hinkley sloop. I've christened him The Commodore. When he's dressed in his yachting togs (and he is a natty dresser), his elegant mustache and imperious bearing make him look like a commodore should look.

> GLADSTONE: I worked with John's father after I came to WOR in 1942, and I still have his rhododendron bushes as a living memory. When John B. operated that nursery in Mt. Sinai, I rented a trailer and drove out there for a load of rhododendron and azalea. They're enormous now. I may have been one of his last customers.
>
> He was a unique personality; there was no one on the air like him. Radio was full of exercise programs, but he was the only one who successfully converted to a general entertainment show. Possibly the secret of his success was that he never did the exercises at all—he urged others to do them.
>
> Young John took a successful program and improved it to serve the needs of the times. Now he has a bigger daytime audience in the metropolitan area than Dick Cavett or Merv Griffin.

I have to include Martha Deane as one of us, even if she comes on the air after 10 o'clock. I feel she is *ex officio* or Our Gang Emeritus because she has been so close to me and Dad over the years.

> MARTHA DEANE: I had been women's editor of Newspaper Enterprise Association, the Scripps-Howard syndicate, before I came to WOR in August, 1941. This was the first job I had in radio, and I was terrified. The station manager gave an order that nobody was to be allowed into

the studio while I broadcast, for fear I would panic and run away. I was simply dreadful, and I knew it.

John B. came in right away and introduced himself. He said he had been listening to my program, and I was going to make it. Stop worrying. And then he did something he'd never done before: He asked me to be a guest on his program. He never had guests.

I got up at 6 A.M. and we talked about me and the job. He went out of his way to put me at ease, to let people know there was a new girl in town. We became good friends, and I used to take his advice on how to manage my life in this radio business.

One day he brought John A. in. He must have been eleven, still in grammar school. I continued to see John A. through the years, when he came in to visit from high school and, later, when he was at Dartmouth.

John A. had a problem with my name. His family had brought him up properly, to call an older woman Miss or Mrs. Since I have a couple of names (my real one is Marion Taylor) and I was much older, he called me Mrs. Taylor for a while. Then, for years, it was Aunt Martha. One day I said, "Why don't you call me Marion—your father does." So for years he called me Martha Marion. Finally, after he took over the show, it became Marion.

I have a nice, easy relationship with John. He is an open, warm person, but you can trust him to keep a confidence. And he relates to people. You can't fool the listening audience. They *know* whether you tell the truth or you're a liar. . . . People in radio often wonder: How can I change my image? You can't. You are what you are. John never had that image problem; he's absolutely on the level. And an enormous number of people like him the way he is. They are his audience.

Well, what can I say after that? Except—meet my audience.

CHAPTER TEN

"IF JOHN GAMBLING SAYS IT, IT MUST BE TRUE"
—Old saying

> Referring to your shaving-lotion ad with "The Lone Ranger and Tonto"—I always heard that Indians never shave because they can't grow beards. So what is Tonto doing, bragging about a shave lotion?
>
> Mrs. Ida M. Milbank
> Rockville Centre, N.Y.

Don't tell Sally, but I'm involved in a love affair with my audience. It's been going on like this for years, but it does create responsibilities and dangers for me. Let me explain.

One of those frequently asked Audience Encounter Group questions is: "When you're sitting there at the microphone, talking to hundreds of thousands of people, what do you *see* in your mind?"

It isn't hundreds of thousands, really. It's a one-to-one relationship. There is only one person at the other end of the kilocycles, not a group. Radio wasn't always this way. If you're over thirty, you can remember when you sat around the radio in your living room with the whole family to hear Edgar Bergen chastize Mortimer Snerd ("How can you be *so* stupid?") and laugh with Charlie McCarthy ("I'll clip ya! So help me, I'll mow ya down!"). It was family night by the radio, perhaps the only radio in the house.

Today radios have proliferated like houseflies. There are more radios (63.9 million) in the U.S. than bathtubs (51.4 million); I'm not sure what that says about the cleanliness of the American people. If there is one thing Americans want, even more than a car in every garage, it's a radio in every room. Or in every car. Or in every ear. And so I visualize Out There one person to one radio—just me and you with only some electronic gadgets in between. You are a composite of suburbanite-apartment-dweller-long-haired-feathercut-single-married-divorced-widowed-college-grad-bluecollar-child-teenager-over thirty-middle-aged-grandparent-male-female. I assure you, it's not easy being in love with a person like that. If you ask me, "What does this composite *look* like?" I must admit, "I don't know."

For one thing, the audience is spread out over a surprisingly large chunk of the United States. WOR's primary daytime coverage includes all of New York City, Long Island, the southeast corner of New York State, Connecticut, Maryland, New Jersey, Rhode Island and Delaware, eastern Pennsylvania, western and southern Massachusetts, and the tiny southernmost tip of Vermont. In the early morning, our signal goes all the way up to Maine and down to Savannah, Georgia. My father tells me that, when the atmospheric conditions are right, he can hear me in Palm Beach, Florida.

We do have several ways of identifying this audience. One is by statistical surveys. Our demographer, Howard Selgar, has come up with an analysis using several different sampling techniques. In an average *Rambling With Gambling* quarter-hour, 6 to 10 A.M., Monday through Friday, the audience can be divided into the following ages and genders:

MEN		WOMEN	
18–24	6,900	18–24	8,300
25–34	21,800	25–34	12,100
35–49	51,500	35–49	106,000
50–64	62,000	50–64	102,300
65+	49,000	65+	112,500
	191,200		341,200

TEENS (male and female) 8,400

TOTAL AUDIENCE: 540,800

And remember, that's just *one quarter-hour*.

Howard has also uncovered even more personal information, based on WOR's average audience, Monday through Sunday, over a twenty-four hour period:

42.5% of the males have an income of $10,000 and over

32.9% of the males have an income of $15,000 and over

93% of the males have a high school education or higher

24.4% of the males went to college

84.9% of the females have a high school education or higher

13.8% of the females went to college

Which indicates that I'd better know my history and geography pretty well, that I can use words of more than one syllable, and even discuss politics, philosophy, and books once in a while. Grunts and "like, oh! wow man!" are not enough.

But cold statistics are only a small part of the audience story.

Let's consider the warm human beings. Here are some actual listeners, picked at random, for interviews. They talked about themselves and why they listen:

MRS. BARBARA HAHN, GLEN ROCK, N.J.: We moved here from the Middle West about thirteen years ago. I had my ear to the radio all morning because I was surrounded by eight children, and I wanted to hear some intelligent adult conversation. My husband, before he left for work, was looking for the time and news and all that. So we turned on Bill Cullen.

After 8 o'clock, when everybody was out of the house except me and the babies, I would have more coffee and listen to Dorothy and Dick. Then we discovered the *Gambling* show. That was before he took over from his father, and I got a little confused between John A. and John B. until eventually I sorted it all out. We became engrossed in the running jokes, and especially the personality of Peter Roberts, whom we love dearly. As a matter of fact, we were going to be out of town one year, and I wrote Peter to ask if we could get the show on another station or TV, but we couldn't.

It's sort of like the show is a member of the family. One son and daughter are away at college now, but they can still hear it; and my husband, who's an engineering manager at Sperry, likes it, too. The younger ones begin to listen at about second- or third-year high school. In their bedrooms, they have rock 'n' roll, but when they come into the kitchen they can't help hear John Gambling, and it has a cumulative effect over the years. They hear it talked about at the dinner table, where we relate some of the jokes we hear. The humor is what we're very much interested in, more than the vital statistics, because we can get that on any other station.

ART ANDROUSKI, EAST 8TH ST., NEW YORK CITY: My shift goes on at 7 A.M., so I have to be out of my place and running by 6:30. I operate an elevator in a high-rise. Gambling's chatter and music sort of tickle me under the chin and put me in a good mood. I mean, nobody particularly likes to get out of bed that early anyhow, but he is cheerful enough for me. Some of those early-show people are *too* breezy—I could throw a shoe at them—and others sound like they really need me to wake *them* up. Gambling is just right. I guess if I didn't have him to wake me up, I'd have to get a wife. But I tell you, my ex was grumbly in the morning and night—so what's the use?

MRS. EUGENE STICKEL, UNION, N.J.: We have a clock radio that wakes me and my husband every morning at 6. He listens, too. Do you think I'd get up that early if I didn't have a husband to make breakfast for? He works for a firm that makes lighting fixtures for the Turnpike.

I've been listening since John was a little boy and used to come on with his father. I recall those exercises, but I was too lazy to do them. I recall when his father announced young John's marriage, and how somebody pushed Dad into the swimming pool at the wedding celebration. I suppose we'll keep on listening as long as he can keep talking. My husband is sixty-eight, and I'm going on seventy.

TIM EDMONDSON, EAST 96TH ST., NEW YORK CITY: Ever since I can remember, I've been listening, because my father and mother had the radio on. There are five of us kids. I'm twelve. Mom usually turns it on when she gets up, which is sometime around 6:30 A.M. I get up at 7 to go to school, so that's when I hear it. All the other people in the house are listening by this time. My youngest sister, Julie, is three. Next one is Katie, who's going to grammar school! she's thirteen. And my oldest sister is sixteen. I listen from 7 to 8. I want to know about the weather, so I'll know what to wear to school. If I don't feel so good, and the weather isn't so good—Mr. Gambling decides me to stay home.

MRS. CONNIE DEL CASTILLO, BECK ST., BRONX, N.Y.: We left Philadelphia after my mother passed on, and my husband got a job here. He'd go to work early, and I felt lonely. I'd turn on my little transistor radio and read at the same time. I like soul music, so, to tell the truth, I don't care much for John Gambling's music. But he's got a lot of soul. Yes, that's true. So much warmth and understanding, he makes me feel like I'm one of the family. I was surprised to hear he's only forty-two years old. I always thought he was older. I work as a domestic now, so I don't have as much time as before, but I turn on his show any odd moment I find on the job.

MRS. VERNE FULMER, BARBERRY RD., WEST ISLIP, N.Y.: We have four radios: one in each bedroom, one in the kitchen, and one is a battery transistor, in case everything else goes off. I sort of half-listen as I go about my housework. When something catches my ear, I concentrate.

Mr. Gambling has a good feeling for words. Because of my work in the school library, I'm very interested in the use of words and grammar. Recently, [name bleeped] said a woman's off-black nylons were "revelatory." That word comes from "revelation" and is concerned with metaphysics and divine truth. The correct word, and much less pompous, is simply "revealing." I also wrote a letter to [name bleeped], who don't seem to know the difference between the verbs "lie" and "lay." In a commercial! If I ever catch John Gambling in that kind of error, I'll write him about it, too.

ARTHUR UNGER, WEST HAVEN, CONN.: I travel to New
York frequently to buy blouses and dresses for my family's
store. Gambling's show has had a strange effect on my
life.

Last year, I was rolling along the Merritt Parkway
listening to his news. At the Stamford entrance, I picked
up a girl hitching to New York. She was a student at the
U. of Connecticut, studying dance; rather moody and
didn't want to talk. Just then, Gambling switched to the
Ray Charles Singers doing "This Can't Be Love" from *The
Boys From Syracuse*. Well, this girl flipped. She was hip
to all the musicals since the thirties; it was her hobby.
Well, that number kept us talking all the way to the city,
because music is one of my interests, too. I drove her
back to Storrs, and the way it worked out, as soon as she
graduates, we're going to get married. I feel he really
introduced us. When the date is set, I hope he can come
to the wedding.

In short, you, my audience, are rather special: affluent, edu-
cated, and over thirty. The more wide-ranging our programming is—the more news, information, and comedy, based on the
day's events—the more we attract this audience. As more and
more young people push on to more and more education, they're
turning to me, too. Trying to please everyone at the same time
is a mirage that only the TV networks can afford to pursue. Our
program concept has produced the largest local radio audience
in the country.

(There is a growing trend in radio that really troubles me.
Prepackaged, computer-programmed tape shows, syndicated for
automatic operation in—so far—about fifty stations around the
country. It's cheaper and easier, of course, and inhuman. The
subscribing station buys programmed music tapes, updated every
week by the syndicator. A computer arranges the "sound" for
the station's market—uptempo for "drive time" or downtempo
at night. You hear the friendly voice of a pretested, prerecorded
disc jockey—but does he ever hear the voice of his audience?
Not likely. *There is nobody in the studio!* It's 2001, thirty years
too soon.)

I know what my listeners want. Service and information. The

weather today: rain, snow, hot or cold. and where, and a little bit of why. What subways are out of commission—what busses are not running on what routes. They want to be amused, they want to be informed of the important news of the day. And they don't want to be troubled by controversy.

Last year, Herb Klein, President Nixon's director of communications, came on my show to answer listeners' phone questions about national policy. The feedback from some of the audience carried a surprise. They were Nixon Republicans, but they objected to politics that early in the morning.

Something else they want: me to be the same every day. It's not easy. We live in a changing, unstable, often unfriendly world. I'm the friendly guy who may be their one secure anchor all day. And that's why, when we make changes in the format, which we sometimes do, we make them gradually, and carefully.

Over the years, I've trained and paced myself so that I sound very much the same for the five hours each morning. But, of course, the show is never exactly the same. I can rarely create what I consider to be a great performance. Every once in a while, I get it all together. I go off the air at 10 and I sigh out loud, "I really did a good one today." I *know* I've been a little funnier, a little brighter. They say football is a game of inches; radio is a game of fractional-wattage sparks, flying in all directions.

Most of my thirty hours a week is solid and professional. There is a level at which a good craftsman becomes an artist like Chippendale. I don't create Chippendale-quality radio very often, but most of my work, I feel, is first-rate craftsmanship. Once in a while, of course, I blow one, and when 10 o'clock comes around I know, deep down, I did a lousy show. Not often, but often enough to keep me trying to do better.

Even above consistency, my audience demands honesty. Since 1925, the *Gambling* show has undoubtedly broadcast more commercials than any show any place in the world. I'm a door-to-door salesman, something like the guy who knocks on your door with the eighty-piece vacuum-cleaner set. He must show you (a) why that vacuum cleaner is better than any other cleaner, and (b) why you need a cleaner. Thanks to the magic of radio (as Mr. Marconi used to say), I get my electronic foot in more doors at one time. I couldn't sell that vacuum if I didn't believe in it.

All our sponsors and their commercials are screened in advance by WOR. Occasionally I find we've misjudged an advertiser or a product—and we throw the commercial off the air. Robert Maley, head of WOR's Continuity Acceptance Department, is a tough watchman.

> MALEY: Over the years we have learned to sniff out something wrong, far in advance. TV has helped radio tremendously by taking over most of the "garbage ads"; somehow those questionable products look desirable on the TV tube.
>
> Most of the advertisers who throw curves seem to be in the home-repair or appliance field: storm windows, house sidings, basement waterproofing. Their guarantees can be tricky. We discontinued one commercial for a siding that could be blown onto the house, over brick, shingles, etc. The guarantee stated, in fine print, that if anything went wrong with the material, the contractor would replace it. And he did deliver the stuff. The only thing the commercial didn't say was that he wouldn't apply it on the side of your house.
>
> Every time we have a few days of heavy rain, the waterproof-basement people swarm onto the air. They don't say much—just announce they are experts in this field and ask you to write for details. The tricky words are in their letter or contract—not in the radio commercial— but we get all the blame anyhow.
>
> We don't accept wild promises: strawberry plants that grow as high as your house, or gasoline additives that give you fifty no-knock miles to the gallon. But a radio station is a handy and visible establishment to gripe to. People get on the phone to complain they don't like the *sound* of the commercial, or the voice of the man making it, or they berate us for commercials that appeared on another station.
>
> It gets pretty wild around here. Some years ago, this woman called in about a commercial for a supermarket:

"They advertised bottom round, $1.10 a pound."

I murmured encouragingly, "Yes. . . ?"

"I went all the way down to the store and brought it home."

"Yes. . . ?" I couldn't figure out what her problem was.

"Now I don't know what to do. Can you tell me how to cook it?"

In commercials—in all of radio—the nitty-gritty is truth. I don't make exorbitant claims for any product. I say, "Here is the product. It does this, and thus and so and thus and so. It costs this much and it is available here. Try it."

Usually, I've tried it first. I operate my own little product testing laboratory. I'll take the new product home to Sally. Or the children. And if we like them, I'll talk about our reactions. Recently a French-fried shrimp came on the market. I took half a dozen packages home and they were very good—tender and tasty, and I said so, on the air. If the product is merely so-so— and not all of them can be great—I'll do the commercial as best I can, without giving it a personal endorsement. If the shrimp had been downright indigestible or tasted like wallpaper paste, I'd have sat down with Bob Maley and considered whether we should run that commercial at all. I'm making a comfortable living, and WOR isn't losing money either, so we don't have to accept every commercial that comes over the transom.

When I talk about a product, my listeners take that as a rec-ommendation. So when it doesn't live up to its claims, the lis-teners don't blame the manufacturer. They blame me. This is, again, that one-to-one relationship, our love affair.

I know what my audience wants because I listen to them. I make an effort to hear them—in their phone calls, letters, in my personal appearances. I'm cut off from the world for five hours a day in a windowless studio. Yet, I'm in the people business. I have to know their needs, goals, anxieties, pleasures. So many people in broadcasting have lost contact with ordinary life; they've shut themselves into the tight little world of New York show business. And they fade away because they're not listen-ing to their audience Out There.

I enjoy working in front of an audience; it's a very warm feeling, where the relationship changes to one-to-many. I'm often a master of ceremonies, holding the program together and introducing the movers and shakers of the sponsoring organization. And my speaking invitations cover a wide cross-section of our society. Looking over a recent calendar: I was scheduled to emcee a National Bible Week lunch at the Waldorf, a money-raising kickoff for the United New York Hospital Fund at a skating show in Rockefeller Center, and to speak at the United Fund dinner in Manhasset, near my home. The egg industry of New Jersey asked me to do six or seven humorous minutes at a dinner honoring the Secretary of Agriculture for that state, an old friend, Phil Alampi. Last year, I was invited to Fairfield University, Fairfield, Conn., to receive their award for Radio Man of the Year.

Unfortunately, I can accept only a very small proportion of the invitations I receive. Working strange hours, time becomes precious: time for my family and time for myself. My weekly calendar will be full from six to eight weeks ahead, as I try to pace myself to fulfill as many business and personal obligations as possible.

I pick my speaking spots in a variety of ways. For some, frankly, I ask a substantial fee. These are primarily business-oriented groups. For charitable organizations, there is usually no fee. Other criteria are the size of the gathering, the time the meeting is scheduled, and the accessibility of the site. But, still, so many times my inclination is to say yes when the demands of my schedule insist no.

If it's a luncheon meeting, I like to talk for fifteen or twenty minutes, then answer questions for ten minutes. The queries are usually similar in all audiences, and rarely critical. They want to know about my two families: my home family (Sally, the children, my parents, the dogs) and my radio family (Peter Roberts and the others on the show).

The ritual of autographing is amusing. I wonder what people *do* with autographs. After I've signed a napkin, postcard, or the back of a letter, are they traded off? Are fourteen of mine worth one of David Frost? I'm pretty sure the napkin is not framed. Occasionally a listener will come up with an autograph book and say, "Will you write a little something to my mother? . . . or daughter?" . . . or, "I told my wife I was going to see you today." So I write, "Best wishes to Helen," and Charlie takes it home to Helen. She looks it over dubiously and asks, "What kind of guy is he?" Then the autograph book is filed away, I guess, with their old theater programs and menus from Miami.

I'm happy to sign autographs. The day nobody wants one, I'll be out of work. Letters are something else. They're the audience's autograph to me.

CHAPTER ELEVEN

THE "DEAR JOHN" LETTERS

I have been listening to radio and your station, WOR, ever since our family was even able to afford a radio. Our first one, sometime in the early 1920s, was an Earl Meisner, one of those with a large horn, two large boxes which I think were the Tuner and Amplifier, two different kinds of Batteries, as we didn't have Electricity yet, plus a separate Aerial which was wound on a Mother Oats container, stretched through two rooms. . . .

Today, you were discussing old-time Radio with Peter Roberts, and you said you didn't know the name of the girl who played in *The Shadow*. It was Margo Laine. You announced that Margo Laine was the girl in the *Superman* series. That is wrong. Lois Lane was the girl in *Superman*.

Anthony Swysz
Red Bank, N.J.

I receive about 100,000 pieces of mail a year, including 1,000 Christmas cards. About half of these are requests: for public-service announcements (church fairs, fund-raising sales, hundreds of charitable ventures) and for items offered on the show (recipe booklets, product information, catalogs, etc.). The other half consists of comments, questions, complaints ("Dear John, you're a faker"), and compliments ("Dear John, you're a friend"). And special requests: for money, help for the sick or mentally ill, research on obscure bits of information. And special offers: recipes, clothing for my children, cures for my cold.

I try to answer them all with a postcard or a letter. I read and sign every answer that goes out. Over the years, some of the questions and requests are repeated so often that Evelyn, my secretary, can answer them for me. She and I have a running gag on these standard answers. We call them "bedbug letters." This is an ancient story involving the president of a large railroad who received an indignant letter from a gentle lady of Boston. She complained that, in her journey to Chicago in one of his Pullmans, she had been bedeviled by bedbugs in her lower berth. She received an elaborate two-page reply. The president was grieved; this had never happened before. The linen was changed twice a day; the cars were cleaned and fumigated every day, as well as the employees. It was such a sweet, humble letter that the lady felt a little ashamed to have brought it up. Then she noticed an interoffice memo, left in the envelope: "Send this old bag the bedbug letter."

Fortunately, *Rambling With Gambling* has very few bugs in it now. But the "form" letters, each written with slight variations, do save time for Evelyn and Marie. They cover about fifty topics, and I write new ones when something on the show provokes an eruption of mail, pro and con. Would you believe:

> *Air pollution and ecology* (one's bad, one's good)
> *Ban on alligator skins and endangered animals for furs* ("there should be a law")
> *Contemporary music* (pro and con)
> *February, pronunciation of* (with or without the first *r*)
> *Grackles and assorted birds* (people write poems)
> *Long vs. short hair* (I'm wearing mine longer)
> *Paul Revere's horse* (a rather specialized discussion)
> *Hunting* (mostly against)

New York City potholes (bigger and deeper)
Christmas music (too soon) (too late)

Evelyn is very adept in these matters; she got her training with
my father:

> EVELYN: A friend of my sister's was working for John B.,
> and she wanted to get married but was afraid he would
> flip if she left him. I was doing bookkeeping for a retail
> coal company in the Bronx—about as far removed from
> radio as you can get—but I said, "Gee, I'd love a job like
> that." Two days later, I had my interview. I'd listened to
> the show since I was a little girl, so I was no stranger to
> the name "Gambling." I told him I hadn't done secretarial
> work for years and my shorthand was rusty; he didn't
> even give me a test. I liked him right off, although he was
> a bit stern. You just didn't fool around with John B. And
> I had some rough moments, because I knew I wasn't
> doing the job I should have. He stuck with me when I
> went back to night school to brush up. At the end of the
> year, I said, "Well, it's our first anniversary." And he just
> looked at me and said, "Lucky was the day you walked
> in that door." When he told me he was retiring, he said,
> "Miss Volpe (he never called me Evelyn), you can pay for
> a stenographer, but you can never pay for loyalty."
>
> I've been with father and son for eighteen years; there's
> a great feeling of continuity, so most of the criticism
> against John A. infuriates me. As he says, it's always
> easier to complain than compliment. When he first
> started, we had many nasty letters accusing him of avoid-
> ing the draft just because he got married when he was
> nineteen. And people said he was an upstart, with no
> talent, and he wouldn't be here if it weren't for his father.
> This kind of mail deserves a tarantula instead of a bed-
> bug letter—but, of course, cranks rarely include their
> address. I have my own theory: Most of the looney letters
> come in when there's a full moon.

They love to catch me in errors of pronunciation or meaning.
Sometimes, I must admit, I fluff a name or date and don't correct
it—sometimes on purpose. It's amazing how many trivia freaks,
like me, there are in this world.

784 Columbus Ave
New York City

I called in the origin of the word "bungalow" this past
Friday, and apparently my voice was nasal and your
assistant misunderstood me. The Hindustani word is
bangla (not *bagla,* as you pronounced it), which means
"of Bengal," and the house that it identifies, with its wide
porch, is native to East Indian architecture. A totally
unrelated but somewhat amusing word origin is that of
"buxom"—which used to mean "obedient" and was from
the Middle English *buhsum* (from *bugan,* "to bend or
bow"), meaning "obedient, flexible, pliant." Thus, a
"buxom and bonny bride" was not necessarily the top-
heavy woman, although maybe the heavier woman tended
to be anchored at home and was therefore more disposed
to being obedient.

This exchange occurred just before East Pakistan became Ban-
gladesh, and *bangla* acquired an emotional political meaning.

Not so long ago, I received a note addressed to the John
Gambling Research Foundation (a nonprofit organization) in-
quiring why it was so much more difficult to shell a hard-boiled
egg today than it was when the writer "was a little girl." And
what was the easiest way?

In our discussion on the air, Peter Roberts had one or two
wild and woolly suggestions, but in the next morning's mail came
the deluge.

> . . . The secret of the perfect egg is to add a few drops of
> vinegar to the water when the eggs are being cooked.

> . . . Add a tablespoon of salt to the water . . . this will stop
> the eggs from cracking.

> If you run cold *water* over them for a few minutes after
> taking them out of the boiling water . . .

> Quick cooling of the shell sounds like excellent physics
> but it just ain't so. I have all this on excellent authority:
> Marion, my wife, who was brought up on a farm in
> Cutchogue, L.I. She knows a good egg when she sees one.
> That's why she married me.

When eggs are allowed to age, uncooked, they slowly decompose. This process produces carbon dioxide. After boiling, eggs that have produced some carbon dioxide will be easy to peel, while a fresh egg will cause the shell and membrane to adhere to the egg white. The problem is, today's eggs are *too fresh*. You have to age them by leaving them out of the refrigerator for a week. . . .

. . . pierce the shell in the widest end, where the air cell is. . . .

Now, any more questions? You'd better take notes, because there may be a short quiz at the end of the chapter.

How would you answer this one?

> West First St.
> Freeport, N.Y.
>
> The other night at the dinner table, my son Bill (age 17½) posed a question. Perhaps you can be of some assistance to my generation.
>
> It seems three men entered a hotel to request a room for the night. The clerk gave them a room for $30, for which each man contributed $10. The clerk, after rechecking, found the rate should have been $25 for the three. He dispatched the bellboy with $5 to be returned to the three men. The bellboy, on the way up, convinced himself that dividing $5 by three was too complicated, so he pocketed the $2 and gave each man $1. Now comes my smartaleck son's question: since each man gave $10 for the room and was refunded $1, their charge was $9. The bellboy pocketed $2, thus making the total $29. What happened to the other $1 from the original $30 involved? HELP! !

Some questions are more personal—and colder.

> If you had to swim in an outdoor pool at swim practice every morning at 10:30 A.M., would you think that 59 degrees is "sunny and pleasant"?

Many unhappy letters come from women accusing me of "male chauvinism." This is a code word used by women's libera-

tionists to label any man who doesn't agree with their dogma.
The lib ladies want to be treated with absolute equality by men,
to which I agree. But I don't believe men and women are the
same. They have different personalities and abilities. I don't say
men are better than women, or that women are better than men.
I say that in the differences there are some inequalities, which
should be corrected. I always treat the subject with a tinge of
humor, because nobody wants serious polemics that early in the
morning. But the complaints come from women totally without
humor. I answer, "When you threw away your bra, you lost
your sense of humor."

> EVELYN: Many complaints are the result of simple mis-
> understanding. People just don't *listen*. They're so busy
> driving a car or baking a pie, they can't concentrate. Re-
> cently, a sponsor ran a contest based on the date appear-
> ing on the label of Kikkoman soy sauce ("Since 1630").
> A woman wrote that she could not find the date. I tried
> to explain exactly where the date appeared, next to the
> word "since." And here is the answer we got:

>> Dear John, As I said before, in my last two letters,
>> I listened to your Dad for many years, since I began
>> working for the New York Telephone Co. forty years
>> ago. So you know I am a senior citizen, and I think
>> I know that when I see the word "since," I can read
>> it. Enclosed is the label on the bottle. Can you see
>> the word "since"?

> Well, she had been looking at the wrong label: not soy
> sauce but the same firm's teriyaki sauce.

The many friendly letters make it all worthwhile. I can't help
being touched by a wistful, yet quirky, correspondent like this:

> N. Amelia Ave.
> DeLand, Florida
>
> Dear John,
>   I miss you! I never thought I'd miss anything in New
> York City (except my few good friends) when I de-
> camped in February for the better life in Florida. . . .

Well, why not—it was an important part of my life for—
my God! how many years?

I would turn you on—that is to say, I'd turn my *radio*
on—at about 5:45 A.M. It's hard to break such a close
association after so many years. Now, even though I'd
love to sleep late, I can't—I'm still awake at 5:45. However, in these parts, radio doesn't come alive until 6 or
6:30, and when it does, it just ain't the same. . . . I miss
you, I miss Petey-baby, I even miss Hennessy, though I
used to want to throw the radio out of the window when
he pronounced it "Lay-oss!"

Why don't you and Petey come to Florida and buy a
radio station and gladden a lady's heart?

I also hear from the people who've moved North.

> Westwood Ave.
> Long Branch, N.J.
> . . . Have been listening to you every morning (while
> having breakfast) since my move here from Florida, and
> it sure beats anything down there. But we haven't the
> faintest idea what anyone on the show looks like. Do you
> send out a photo or scorecard, so I can tell the players
> apart?

Friendship knows no age:

> Nixon Drive
> Kenvil, N.J.
> 8:35 A.M.
> You're a dear! I wonder what you are doing when you
> and Mr. Roberts fool around. I think you should call
> yourself *Grumbling With Gambling*. Love from—
> Regina, age 3½
> (dictated to Mother)

> N. Oration Parkway
> East Orange, N.J.
> Sir, I am ninety-five years old and hear your program on
> WOR quite often, as I have ever since your dad started
> to broadcast. . . . I remember your granddad from Cam-
> bridge, England, and how he wore a heavy suit of clothes

while on a visit here. And you going to Glen Ridge to see the daughter of the auto agent whom you married and is now your wife. . . . Meatpackers used to use all the carcass of pigs except the squeal; now they put the squeal on records and call it music.

"I miss you!" and "You're a dear" and "Love you dearly" appear in many letters. I occasionally receive perfumed notes from women suggesting a rendezvous in the Plaza Palm Court or even the Biltmore. My father did, too.

> JOHN B.: This gal in Connecticut would write a thick letter about once a week, and each one would describe a meeting with me. All imagined, of course—she was married. She would tell how I'd meet her at Grand Central and we'd taxi to the Waldorf for a weekend. She went into minute detail of what we accomplished in the hotel. And next week, she'd switch to the Plaza. I showed my wife one of the cooler letters, because if she had ever found them in my office, she'd never believe me. Eventually, I burned them.

Several years ago, I was plagued by an unfortunate woman who kept sending expensive gifts, all charged to my name at New York department stores. I suppose she felt she could make me feel obligated to her by such gifts, yet couldn't afford to buy them. I returned these packages to the stores, which were reasonably understanding; but she continued sending others. Finally, I turned the matter over to Jim McAleer, our program manager, and he got in touch with her husband. End of sad soap opera.

When Sarah Jane was very young, we received hand-crocheted booties and layettes. My family continues to be a favorite subject for correspondents.

> Brear Ave.
> Toms River, N.J.
> I want to take this time to wish your daughter Sarah Jane a very happy birthday. It is one birthday I'll never forget (August 13). Our daughter was born on the same

day. I remember you mentioning your daughter's birthday while I was riding to the hospital. . . . I listened to your program all the way, and did a lot of praying, too! God was good to us. We finally got our girl after three boys.

After I brought home a kitten, purchased at an auction, I had a torrent of suggestions for names. One offered the name of her pet, now deceased—Useless Mahoney. The demise of an old willow tree in our backyard evoked an "Ode to Your Willow Tree" from a gentleman in Hackensack, N.J.:

> Poor willow—weeping from its mouth;
> Poor willow—leaning to the south.
> Big raindrops—shallow with respect:
> How did you ever stand erect?
> Poor willow—weakened at its mouth;
> Poor willow—fallen to the south.

My occasional hoarse throat or cold sends listeners into a frenzy of ingenuity, even topping the destruction of gypsy moths or peeling of eggs. They suggest "hot baths and horehound drops . . . 5,000 units of vitamin C every day. . . . Take the skin of a frog caught by moonlight and grind it. . . ." For colds, I generally end up going to my doctor, who prescribes antibiotics. For hoarseness, I find the best remedy is plain tea, laced with honey. Not brandy. Brandy at 5 in the morning simply makes you *think* you sound better.

The mail is loaded with humor: attempts, complaints, or gifts of:

> Just thought you'd like some cute quotes.
> 1. Knowledge is power, but it won't make the car go.
> 2. Golf is a game that begins with a golfball and ends with a highball.

From 1964 to 1969 I was the target of kooky monthly postcards signed by "Alice Kaputt" (from the German *alles kaputt,* I suppose, meaning "all is lost" or "it's all over").

The postmark was Port Washington, N.Y., near my home. I

enjoyed her puns, read them on the air, but never discovered
who she (or could it have been he?) was.

My friend, ANNA LITTIKOL, asks me to tell you that
she certainly does recall PFC. HY BRACKETTS when
they worked together at the Gross Income Division, under
GENERAL LEDGER'S command at Fort Taxation. She
wonders whether HY remembers the Old Gang in Exemp-
tions: Major deZASTER, Corporal PUNISHMENT and
Private LEE OWNED.

> Your friend,
> Alice Kaputt
> Mon.-Fri., 8:15-9 A.M.

I don't know why she stopped. I've saved all the cards, and
may someday publish *The Strange Case of Alice Kaputt.*

Of course, I never expected to hear a complaint that our show
was *too* funny!

> Box 546, GPO
> New York City.

. . . George Meade [our second helicopter pilot] is going
to be the death of me yet. On Friday morning, when he
flipped with, "I want a big fat mama to tell my troubles
to," he cracked me up so, I had to pull off to the side of
the L.I. Expressway to recover. That boy is way out!

Humor, like Gershwin's woman in *Porgy and Bess,* is a sometime thing.

*

Just the mention of a pet—a cat, a dog, a fish, or man's best
friend, the aardvark—will touch off a series of anecdotes, memories, and pet peeves.

> Cedar Street
> East Hanover, N.J.

The other morning, one of you read an article about left-
handed dogs and cats, and you didn't believe it. Let me
add something, too. . . . As of today, we have twenty cats
and dogs, all spayed or neutered, and a small Chihuahua

dog. Out of this group, I have three cats who shake paws
left-handed, and pick up their last morsels of Purr mini-
bits out of their dishes. All the other cats shake right-
handed. . . . Does Peter Roberts still have his cat that
can tell the weather?

> Merritt Drive,
> Oradell, N.J.

On Tuesday, Peter Roberts says that dogs are unable to
eat Jello. As a biology teacher, I felt I had to verify this
for myself. . . . We do not own a dog, but I did have Jello
in the refrigerator. My sons brought a plate of Jello to a
neighbor's dog, and he did eat every bit of it with enjoy-
ment.

> Ramapo Ave.
> Pompton Lakes, N.J.

. . . This then is the situation. Our dogs are afraid of cats,
and our cat is afraid of birds! Our children seem reasonably well-adjusted, but tell me—where have we failed
our pets?

> E. 11th St.
> New York City

I heard you and Peter discussing waterbeds this morning,
and I wonder if you have any serious, scientific advice on
my idea. My waterbed is transparent plastic. I am also a
tropical-fish fancier, with some rare and very colorful
specimens: purple, bronze, cerise. I'd like to put them in
the waterbed for a really colorful, unusual effect.

Sounds great. A sleep-in fishtank.

My audience not only wants advice—they're eager to give it,
on any subject.

> N. Quaker Hill Road
> Pawling, N.Y.

. . . Despite Dr. Bob's optimistic weather predictions for
the last weekend, we knew better and were prepared for
rain! Here's how: Each morning, as my husband and I
drive up to our store in Kent, Conn., we pass a dairy farm
in Sherman. The cows are out in pasture and visible from
the road. . . . When the majority are lying down, it means
rain within twenty-four hours. Standing cows mean good

weather ahead. We have found the cows to be surprisingly accurate in their forecasts. Perhaps Dr. Bob could
use a pasture of cows to aid him.

I did a phone interview with a morning disc jockey in Oregon
who told me he predicted the weather by watching wild goats on
a nearby hillside. That got Dr. Bob's goat, I'm afraid, but the
guy claimed the goats were 80 percent accurate.

The letters fall like a heavy snow after an outrageous fluff—
booboo or blooper, call it what you will. Bill McEvilly tells this
one best.

> MCEVILLY: John says that thirteen is his lucky number.
> Well, this happened on a Friday the thirteenth, when he
> and Peter Roberts were recording one of their "funnies"
> to be used the following Saturday. They do the taping
> during a news break, between 8 and 8:15. They started
> one tape and messed it up, which doesn't happen too
> often. They began a second tape at 8:09, dangerously
> close to airtime. The engineer had the "air" key set, ready
> to go on at 8:15. John was unhappy about the second
> tape and groaned, loud and clear to Peter, "Well, I guess
> we f - - - - d that up!" Unfortunately, John's back was
> turned to the control room, and just as he said it, the
> "on the air" light lit up. I died. The engineer went pale.
> Fred Feldman, in the helicopter, screamed on our inter-
> com, "What'd he say? What'd he say?" The phone oper-
> ator called in absolute panic—she was already getting
> "Good heavens!" calls from outside. John spun around in
> his chair and immediately knew what had happened.
> We all recovered pretty quickly, but I'll always remember
> Fred yelling incredulously, "What'd he say?"

The incident created all sorts of havoc—discussion with management, letters of explanation to the FCC, and, for my part, a
terrible feeling of chagrin that something as stupid as this could
really happen.

I got a lot of letters, but with very few exceptions they were
understanding, amusing, and amazingly tolerant. In fact, one
listener wrote that the whole incident made me much more
human.

There's an old maxim in broadcasting that you should never say anything out loud in a studio that you don't want to go over the air. I suppose it is remarkable that this "unspeakable" language isn't heard more often. Taped TV shows have their edited bleeps, but live radio has only red faces.

I guess the best-known open-mike fiasco is attributed to Don Carney, who was known as Uncle Don, some thirty years ago. He broadcast a children's show from the same WOR studio I use today . . . which may have some significance. As the story goes, Don thought the show had ended and muttered, "That'll hold the little bastards for tonight!" A flood of letters is supposed to have ended his career. But, to the best of my knowledge, he never said it.

My authorities are (1) his biography, published some years ago, and (2) my father, who knew Don well. The tale became nationally known on a record of so-called famous bloopers, but that was a re-enactment, a staged stunt.

My father fell into a genuine but innocent booboo years ago. He would have the orchestra play the dwarfs' march from Disney's *Snow White* ("Heigh-ho, heigh-ho, it's off to work we go") to shoo people off to their jobs in a happy state of mind. One St. Valentine's Day, he dramatized the occasion by visualizing the dwarfs in the studio: "And there go Grumpy and Sneezy and the other five dwarfs off to work this Valentine's Day, each with a big red heart on. . . ." Chaos!

Johnny Cook told me he and Dad were ready to head for the hills. But the letters were understanding. Among them was an obviously feminine note, in red ink: "Lucky Snow White!"

Peter Roberts pulled a funny one unconsciously (that's when he's best) on a 6:30 news broadcast. The Russians had sent some live germs up in one of their early space probes. Peter reported that "the Russians are testing the effects of space travel on living orgasms. . . ."

In the studio, Johnny Cook and McEvilly waved their arms and roared. I was in the studio, and just folded up under the U-shaped desk. Peter, always the total professional, stopped for just a fraction of a second and, without the barest trace of a

smile, said, "I beg your pardon. That should be 'organism.' "
Beautiful.

I should not have been surprised by his imperturbability. Before he came to WOR, he had been a newscaster at WINS, where he had to fend off daily attacks of madness instigated by Bob and Ray. These zanies would do anything to break up poor old Pete. They succeeded so often that the station management, upset by the image of their premier newsman laughing his way through world-shattering news, ordered Peter to work from a separate studio. Bob and Ray were forbidden to enter it while he was on the air.

Ray discovered that their studio and Peter's shared an air-conditioning duct. By standing on a chair, he and Bob could shout obscenities into the ventilator . . . muffled enough not to be heard on the air but just clear enough to break up lovable old Petey.

Management ordered the two comics to stay away from the ventilator—in fact, they were threatened with extreme penalties if they ever came *near* Pete while he was broadcasting. They promised they wouldn't. A couple of days later, a most attractive young woman walked into Peter's studio. Noiselessly, she stepped between him and the control-room glass . . . and noiselessly took off all her clothes. I've been told it is difficult to deliver a newscast with your head scrunched down over the script, hands cupped over the head to shade the eyes—and body convulsed with laughter.

A booboo I made on an American Motors Rambler auto commercial was mildly traumatic. I said, "There's always good nudes with a new Rambler." Most of the letter-writers kept their shirts on. Except for the one who said he stripped his gears.

I also have the distinction of delivering two perfect spoonerisms. These are twists of the tongue that transpose sounds or words and are named after the Rev. William Spooner, an Englishman noted for such blunders.

One was a commercial for the Robert Hall clothing chain, extolling the benefits of a short coat for boys, a "melton benchwarmer." It came out as a "menton belchwarmer."

Another popped out in an ad for Richardson & Robbins-brand chicken fricassee. I remember joking with Bill McEvilly about the wild possibilities for error in their commercial, so I made a mental note—*watch it*. Sure enough, a million people heard me call it "friggin chickassee!"

My list of spoonerisms goes back at least twenty years. I was a shaky, green kid at WTSL in Lebanon, N.H., when I introduced vocalist Peggy Lee as Leggy Pee.

In spite of these lapses, a listener was inspired to write to the president of Dartmouth College, complimenting the school for graduating me.

> . . . If Dartmouth is responsible for Mr. Gambling's flaw-less diction and perfect English, and I am sure it is, I want to congratulate you. He has every mark of a well-educated gentleman. . . . Apparently Dartmouth equipped Mr. Gambling well—the foundation was laid at Hanover and he has not failed you. It is indeed refreshing to hear gentlemen speak well and convincingly.

*

My letters resound with pleas, cries, even demands for help!

> I am a night watchman at a factory in North Branch, and I am a great fan of the old railroad steam-engine era. I love the sound of a steam whistle coming around the bend. Would it be possible to dig up some of these old whistle records?

Answer: Sorry, alarm clocks are bad enough in the morning. Train whistles would be too much.

> Lately, it is impossible to hear your show because of a man with a "ham" radio station. He comes over the air as "Skippy," and his call letters are Metro 429. I have in-formed federal communication agencies, but can't get any relief. Can you do something to shut him up for a few hours?

Answer: Tell Skippy to stick to his peanut butter and stay off our frequency. (WOR wrote to the FCC.)

... I have a page taken from the magazine section
of the *Sunday News*, May 8, 1955, showing a collection
of horses of Mr. J. Allen Williams. I wrote the paper for
his address—no answer.

I would appreciate if you could put me in touch with
Mr. Williams, as I would like to dispose of a meerschaum
cigaret holder of beautiful workmanship. Also a small
piece which does not have the mouth attached. This is a
lady's head with hat and front to waistline. The large
holder is a lovely group having a horse, a soldier on him,
a small boy, a lady holding a spread-out fan, and a dog
barking at the horse. ...

Answer: None. There are times when it's better to drop back
ten yards and punt.

Every day's mail brings its quota of requests for money. The
needs are as varied as the handwriting. Some charitable organizations request articles of clothing so they can auction them off to
raise money; I usually send record albums that I've autographed.
(Some radio celebrities actually send old ties. I've got plenty of
these, all striped, but who would want them?) I usually will not
send a cash contribution; I have my own program of contributions to schools, churches, and community groups in which I
have a personal interest.

Every day also brings its quota of offers. I am constantly delighted by the number of people who want to do something for
me.

I would like to help liven up your show. I am a published
poet for many years. My poems are light and easy listening, and hold all audiences.

Answer: Sorry, but I'm holding my own. (I am constantly
amazed at how many amateur poets there are in the world. And
they all seem to listen to me.)

I have been a successful *money-finder*, and I can teach
this art to you. I obviously excel, but my nine-year-old
daughter has surpassed me. We donate our found funds
to charity. We have mastered the art of surreptitiously

checking phone booths, including the area under the seat, shelf and behind the door; the ground around bus stops and toll booths (but never get out on the highway to check phone booths unless you are desperate), the floors around theater-ticket and candy counters, near cash registers and coat racks (things fall from pockets). Nooks and crannies around checkout counters and supermarket aisles must be checked. . . . In a crowded situation, it's best to drop a handkerchief or something, to give you an excuse to bend down and look around. Always check deep seats in which individuals with jangling pockets have been seated. . . . I would be *curious to hear your reactions.*

Having listened to, and enjoyed, many interesting broadcasts by you and your father, I enclose a photostat copy of an old Marriage Certificate.
It reflects the marriage of my grandfather and grandmother by the Mayor of New York City on November 17, 1851. I am *curious to get your reaction.*

Well, my reactions are getting curiouser and curiouser. Especially after a letter took me to task for using "curiouser and curiouser" on the air. Ungrammatical, the writer said. The phrase comes, of course, from Lewis Carroll's *Alice in Wonderland,* and my only justification for using it is—after a hard day among my letters, I know exactly how Alice felt.

Now let me tell you how I feel about sponsors.

CHAPTER TWELVE

THE DAY OF THE FLYING BLINTZES

It's a miserable day. No chance for golf. The squirrels are at my bird feeder. What could be more appropriate than to adopt the attitude that misery loves company and let some otherwise unoffending friend have it.

. . . Do you suppose that banshee who shrieks [slogan for a car commercial] accomplishes anything but to drive listeners to hide their heads under the covers? . . . Wouldn't it be an improvement if the commercial stated—if you buy one of our cars and the frappis cappastatis fails in any weather, just mail the car back to the factory in the original carton, and the trouble will be corrected at no cost?

Charles E. Humiston
Bernardsville, N.J.

Most sponsors are likable. And very necessary. Without sponsors, American radio would be much, much duller and less variegated than it is. Our industry is different from any other country's. It is government-licensed, privately owned and profit-oriented. That's what gives radio its infinite variety of form, taste—and sponsors.

Here is an interesting, objective view of our show by a visitor from another planet: England, where radio is government-controlled and operated. Daniel Wolf, a young TV and radio writer,

spent a day with me as part of his research into the phenomenon
of American radio.

> WOLF: The only comparable show in England is *Today*,
> from 7 to 9 A.M. It is anchored by Jack DiManio, who's
> been on thirteen years. His style is somewhat less infor-
> mal than Gambling's but, paradoxically, much more
> "folksy" in language.
>
> He does not offer services such as traffic or weather
> reports. It's mainly amusing entertainment features about
> people in the news; nothing political. Since there is very
> little music and no commercials, each item may run five
> or six minutes.
>
> News reports in the U.S. are longer than ours, but there
> is no banter on *Today* with the "news readers." England,
> so far, has fewer cars on the road, and their drivers do
> not constitute a special audience.
>
> Two hours is considered a long time for any European
> show.

That's radio without commercials. WOR permits a maximum
of eighteen minutes of commercial time per hour. But eighteen
times five hours per day times six days a week times fifty-two
weeks a year times lots of years equals many, many commercials. And many, many sponsors.

One group of sponsors just *happens*. They are on the commercial list each morning, year in and year out. The bread-and-
butter ads: gasoline refiners and retailers, major airlines, beer
companies and soft-drink bottlers. They buy big. They buy
many stations, many programs all over the country. They buy
by the numbers. They take the audience ratings of a given show,
calculate these figures in terms of the cost of the time (*Rambling
With Gambling* charges up to $260 per minute), and if the ratio
fits in with the ad agencies' buying plans—they buy.

These clients are the backbone of our business, but it is rare
when my personal contact with this kind of advertiser is more
than a letter to the advertising director or the ad-agency account
executive, expressing my appreciation for their business. Although the percentages may vary from year to year or season to

season, this kind of "big buy" advertiser accounts for about one-third to one-half of our total morning business.

Then there are the other sponsors, the men and women I meet personally. They are often owners of the company that's advertising, or top-management people, or the head of a small ad agency for whom the account is very important.

We have a meeting. It's a first-name proposition right from the start. We talk about the advertiser's problems, his product, his competition. Specifically, what can *Rambling With Gambling*—what can *I*—do to help sell his product?

I know my morning audience's habits, likes, and dislikes very well. And often this knowledge can help shape and plan the sponsor's campaign. The WOR account executive, whose client this is, also sits in on these meetings, and together we often help the advertiser with copy, with personal letters from me to his dealers, and other on- and off-the-air sales tools.

Most businessmen are totally involved in their product: They eat and breathe their no-iron pajamas or grated parmesan cheese. Shaking up their conventional one-way-tunnel vision of how to market the product takes a lot of persuasion. I recall a meeting with the executives of the Homelite Company, which manufactures a special type of gasoline-powered saw to cut trees, wood planks, or logs. The WOR salesman explained how our audience's interests, age, geographic distribution, and income created a perfect market for chain saws. All the while, half listening, I was glancing through a survey made by the Albert Sindlinger organization, which had analyzed our audience. I like to shake up these meetings anyhow, so I interrupted:

"Do you know, gentlemen, that WOR has more unemployed men listening to it than any other station in the country?"

There was a slightly embarrassed laugh. And a pause for re-grouping. My point was not absurd: People with time on their hands would be inclined to work around the house, cutting down unwanted trees. And, in spite of my quirky sense of salesmanship, we got the account.

My sponsors are willing to make a few adjustments for me. To "finalize" a project, two-and-a-half-hour luncheon meetings,

with sustaining martinis, are *de rigueur*. I've been up since
3 A.M.; by noon or 1 P.M. my circadian body rhythm tells me it
is midnight. I'm tired. I'm ready for a nap. So we meet at WOR
or in the sponsor's office after I finish taping my Saturday segments—about 11 A.M. Then the WOR account exec, the agency
people, and the client go out to lunch. And I go home to sleep.

I will often visit the sponsor's factory or showroom for a tour.
One of the joys of my business is the opportunity to see the
hidden wheels of a great many other businesses. The "boss's-eye
view." A little knowledge, of course, can be a dangerous thing.

The president of Milady's Blintzes gave me the deluxe guided
tour of his brand-new, fully automated, air-conditioned plant
in Brooklyn. (For the uninitiated, blintzes are a variation of the
French crêpe: thin pancakes wrapped around a filling of fruit,
cheese, or potato.) I've always been fascinated by the intricacies
and inventiveness of automatic machinery that prepares or packages a zillion of this or that per hour. As we reached the station
on the production line where the fillings are squeezed into the
pancakes, something went haywire. The machinery began blow-
ing blintzes all over the place. Blueberries spraying in one di-
rection, mashed potatoes in another, and dough arching over all,
like a mortar barrage. It was a blintz blitz. They had to shut
down the machinery, and we all went out to an elaborate lunch.
Steak—not blintzes.

At the C. F. Mueller Co. plant in Jersey City, where they
produce tons and tons of pasta, entire boxcar loads of flour are
dumped into giant bins at the top of the factory. They add water
and whatever on the way down; the dough is pushed through
a mold of little holes, baked, and it comes out as miles and miles
of spaghetti. Oversimplified maybe, but fascinating.

I've watched them put together the Sau-Sea frozen shrimp
cocktail in Yonkers, N.Y. Again, a new, immaculate plant. The
shrimp are cooked in giant cauldrons, then frozen with the sauce
in small glasses. What they can't bottle is the smell of hundreds
of gallons of shrimp a-cooking. But I didn't lose my appetite.

And I've learned how they make the vermouth that goes with
the martini that goes with the shrimp. The Tribuno people bring

white wine in railroad tank cars from California to their establishment in Lodi, N.J., where I watched it blended with aromatic herbs and spices. The one man in the world who has the secret of the blend under his hat, according to the ads, is John Tribuno. And there really is a John Tribuno, I discovered—a pleasant, courtly gentleman. He showed me around and plied me with samples, but wouldn't take off his hat.

I always try to sample the sponsor's product. Howard Samuels, head of the Offtrack Betting Corporation, touted me onto the $2 tour before their first office opened. He answered a lot of questions on the mechanics of betting the horses, but he didn't hand out any free samples. I opened an OTB phone account to wager a bob now and then. (I'm strictly a hunch bettor.)

Lots of banks advertise with us. I meet the president and chat about how beautifully they store the money and isn't it wonderful how their dividends grow, compounded quarterly, half-yearly, even monthly or every second. They never send me any samples, either. I know something about their problems, because for about six years I've been a director of the Hempstead Bank in Long Island. It has branches in Nassau and Suffolk counties and has given me a nodding acquaintance with the world of finance.

Occasionally, sponsors send samples right to the studio. Le Chambertin restaurant once popped in about 6 A.M. with a tray of hot apples, each baked in a pastry shell and topped with a strawberry, to the delight of the morning crew. The Jersey apple-growers deliver a few baskets in season—to assure me the formula of their product hasn't changed. And American Airlines has ferried in trays of an ambitious new meal they were testing, complete with stewardesses. We also get samples before the product appears on the air: cookies, ice cream, frozen spinach, and other such diet-busters.

Some people have the mistaken notion that advertisers supply us broadcasters with products, not only for the duration of the ad campaign but for life. This fantasy is as far-fetched as my owning WOR. Freeloading on the sponsor is payola, which is a dirty word in radio. RKO-General and WOR are very specific

in their objections to it. All on-the-air talent must sign an affi-
davit that their outside business activities do not create a "conflict of interest." Which means: Don't use your position at
WOR to make private take-home arrangements.

To sample the real-estate developments that want to advertise,
I talk to the people living there, get the feel of the environment.
My father broadcast commercials for Florida properties years
ago. Now the most popular development is the retirement village. Getting there is half the fun. A few years ago, the advertiser asked me to come visit Leisure Village, near Lakewood,
N.J. To make it easier, Fred Feldman ferried me in Helicopter
710. And he proved that he's not called Fearless Fred just for
alliteration. After a pleasant lunch and stroll around the property
the rains came. A 100- to 200-foot ceiling. "No problem," said
Fred. "Neither rain nor snow et cetera can stop me from the
swift completion of my appointed rounds. And getting J.G.
home for his nap."

We took off from Lakewood, heading east in search of the
Atlantic coastline. Fred adroitly avoided some high-tension lines
by climbing ten feet and losing visual contact with the ground.
Down we went again, slowly following the beach north to
Sandy Hook, hanging just over the breakers. The beach ends
at Sandy Hook, and the Lower Bay was completely socked in
with rain and fog. How to navigate to the city and Long Island?
I'd sailed our boat, the *JAG*, in this bay, navigating by the sea
buoys. I volunteered to do it by air. Fred didn't flinch.

We dropped down to the water, hunting for buoys to guide
us. We passed a Moran tug, and I had an eyeball-to-eyeball
confrontation with the astonished captain at the wheel. It was
a jaundiced eye. But we made it to the 30th Street heliport. Fred
announced, "You were so busy watching the water, you didn't
even notice the Verrazano Bridge."

"Why? Did we fly close to it?"

"No. *Under* it."

Fred may be a major in the Air Force Reserve, but I rib him
about being a minor in navigation. Take the time he flew me
down to Freehold Raceway in New Jersey, another advertiser,
for a gala promotional trot called "The John Gambling Pace."

All that means is, I get to make the award to the winning driver. No tips on the race.

Fred picked me up at 30th Street and we veered south toward our old friend, the Lower Bay and the Statue of Liberty. Here he turned to me: "I guess you know where you're going?"

"You're the pilot," I answered. "I haven't the foggiest notion of how we get there."

"Well," he said, "*somebody* in this bird has to know the way."

I had stashed a roadmap in my briefcase mostly as a gag. No joke this trip. I rummaged around, and by the time I had spread it out on my knees and found north, we were south of Perth Amboy and, as the kids say, cruising.

"All right, Fred, take a sharp right turn here, and we ought to hit the Jersey Turnpike." He obligingly dipped down to about fifty feet so we could read the signs pointing to the entrance. We rode the Turnpike until it intersected with Route 33 at Hightstown. "Now sharp left, Fred, and after 33 intersects with the Garden State, we're in Freehold."

We hit it right on the nose and made a grand entrance, landing on the grass in the middle of the track. And we didn't even pay Turnpike tolls. That was 1967. In the years since then, I've introduced Fred as the hot pilot who needs road maps.

Last fall we made the same excursion. When we were over the Lower Bay, Fred turned to me again: "All right. You've taken flying lessons. Now let's see you navigate to Freehold, *without* a road map."

I shook my head sadly. "You mean, after five years, you still haven't learned the way?"

"Navigate!"

I pinpointed our destination and he landed right on target.

What I don't understand is, how does Fred find his way from the George Washington Bridge to the Bruckner Traffic Circle in the Bronx—all alone?

*

Advertisers can be demanding. Over the years, I've done my share of supermarket openings. I've pulled the lucky numbers for the silver salad-serving sets. I've signed as many autographs and squeezed as many hands as a freshman candidate for Congress. Even if the store advertises my name in letters a foot high and fiery red, there is always a harried mother in slacks, hair curlers under a scarf, who glares at me while she asks the checkout clerk, "Who is *that?*"

As if I'm the mysterious fellow who goes around raising the prices.

Firms that want to break into the New York market face a formidable problem: What's the use of advertising on the radio if your product isn't even on the shelves? And shelf space is always at a premium. The usual answer is: Nudge the stores into stocking the product. This is done with a standard radio commercial plus the suggestion: "If you can't find SuperSoup in your favorite store, ask the manager to order it for you. He *can!*" Of course, this will generate only one sale. After that, the soup must be super enough to create a second and third sale.

Most advertising campaigns run for thirteen-week cycles; only a few advertisers stay on for a full year or more. It's a great personal satisfaction to me when a sponsor comes back to the program after a hiatus of a few months with a new campaign. It's even more satisfying when our show helps build some rather unique business successes.

Consider Philomena Marsicano. She had been an admiralty lawyer; her mother operated the beauty shop in the Plaza Hotel. After her mother died in 1963, Philomena sold that business. But . . .

> PHILOMENA MARSICANO: I was very close to Mother. I used to come in late in the afternoon and chat with her until she closed up. She'd made so many friends among her customers. When she died, I felt a void. I wanted to carry on her work. I'd given up my law practice, so I took over a shop at 26 West 38th St., named it Antoinette's Beauty Salon—her name was Antoinette.
>
> When I first started advertising on John's show, I have to admit I wasn't sure I was going to stay with him. It was six months before I noticed any change; at least we were making expenses. But I liked the caliber of women who were brought in by his program.

He does things *nobody* else would think of. A woman
wrote him about two beautiful Siamese cats in our shop.
He read the letter on the radio, and I can't tell you how
many people came in to see the cats! We've been spending
about $1,000 a week on ads, and business has increased
400 percent in those nine years.

I still have time for my other interests. My German
shepherd dog had no place to run in the city, so I bought
some land in Goshen, N.Y. I had to put up a fence to
keep the dog in. Then, to make the fence pay, I put in
thirty-one head of thoroughbred Charolais cattle. For
breeding. And I just took a ninety-nine-year lease on a
building at 435 Fifth Ave.; the shop will move there in
1973. . . . I wouldn't stay in business without John. I
should insure his life.

I wish I could insure her admirable energy. Philomena is sixty-
six.

My career was shaped by two Bobs; here's a sponsor who
feels two G's have kept him in business.

AL COOPER: One G is the new Garden [Madison Square],
the other is Gambling. They did my steakhouse a world
of good. Of course, I was doing all right before. I've been
in this location in Herald Square for twenty-six years,
ever since I came out of the infantry in 1945. I advertised
on other radio shows, I had lots of celebrities come in
here, I had plugs in Walter Winchell's column. Fine.
About eight years ago, I got on a three-a-week schedule
with John and—it's a little hard to believe. In spite of the
Nixon "boom" (some call it "recession") about a hundred
people a night come in and tell me they heard John
recommend us. I think he must account for 25 percent
of my business. One man said to me, "The way Gambling
recommends you, he must be your partner."

"He gets enough money to be my partner," I said.

They're business people, tourists, whole families, Wall
Streeters. Very substantial. A lot of them ask, "What does
John Gambling like?"

I have to tell them he likes to come into the kitchen.
He likes to look into the refrigerator. He *likes* cleanliness.
I think he's checking to see if all my stainless steel is
really stainless.

I've got a big staff here. Eight chefs, three hatcheck girls; one waiter and one busboy to every two tables. If John ever leaves WOR, I'll have to go with him. We'll all go.

One sponsor holds the record for long-distance waiting. He wanted to get on my father's show eighteen years ago. Dad was advertising Chambers' furs, and at the time WOR gave the client exclusivity; that is, no competitor's products could appear on the same show. So Sid Benjamin (Flemington Fur Co.) waited and waited.

SID BENJAMIN: I'd been listening to John B. for many years. When I couldn't get him, I settled on Martha Deane, and we still have her. But I had my heart set on Gambling. After a few years, Chambers went out of business—and another furrier, the Ritz Thrift Shop, came on John's show. I was out in the cold again. But I hung in there, waiting, for seven years. Until WOR dropped its exclusivity policy. At last I made *Rambling With Gambling*.

I've forgiven John for keeping me waiting at the church so long, and we've become good friends. We're the same age, we play the same kind of golf—not great but better than average. We play two or three times a year, sometimes with Joe Costa, the ice cream man, who's another advertiser. Everybody's happy.

That's the best kind of sponsor. Happy.

Like his mother and father, our son John married his high-school sweetheart. Christine is teaching nursery school while John finishes at the School of Communications, Boston University.

Ann was married to Chris Janelli on August 12, 1972. This is a favorite photograph of mine, as Sarah Jane and Sally beam during a fitting of Ann's wedding dress.

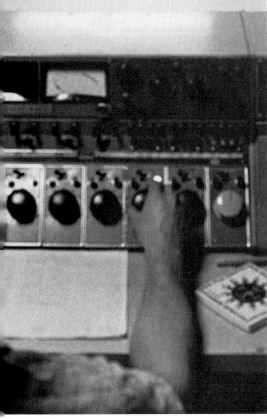

The view from the control room, Studio 2, WOR-AM. I usually work in shirt sleeves. Only newscasters wear jackets.

The U-shaped desk in Studio 2 is littered by the middle of a busy morning. Coffee cup, commercials, cartridges for music, telephone, and a tiny earphone tucked in my ear so I "hear" what's going out over the air.

I hope *you* will be listening to-morrow morning.

This recent picture of my mother and father was taken beside their pool in Palm Beach, Florida. The Sunshine State has been home since Dad's retirement.

Sailing, golf, skiing, and tennis are the sports which Sally and I have been able to enjoy together, joined as often as possible by the children. Although *JAG* was a power boat, our most recent cruises have been under sail.

The family all together. From the top of the ladder
. . . Sarah Jane and Ann, then Ann's husband, Chris
Janelli . . . our daughter-in-law, Christine, and our son,
John. Sally and I are being upstaged as usual by our
Newfoundland, Little Bear's Nana.

CHAPTER THIRTEEN

PRIVATE LIVES: "I GO TO BED WITH YOUR HUSBAND"

> I always thought from your voice you were very sexy. Today I received your photograph. . . .
>
> A Former Admirer
> N. Adams, Mass.

SALLY: I could always adjust to John's strange working hours, but some of the weird feedback from his shows was unsettling. When he did *Music From Studio X* late at night, I'd meet charming women who smiled and announced, "You know, I go to bed with your husband every night." When he began *Rambling With Gambling*, women would tell me, "I'm in the bathroom with your husband every morning." Corny and funny, but a little irritating, too. For a while I had the eerie feeling that thousands of unknown women were coming between me and John. My fantasy groupies. . . . Now, when I hear a variation of the old theme—"I wake up with John"—I say, "Great! I hope you will every morning."

The show, so personal to so many listeners, must intrude in the lives of my family. I do my best to maintain our privacy with the weapons at hand: a sense of humor, a sense of family, and active sports.

I don't involve my family in the show as much as my father did. Young John once toddled home from the second grade to ask Sally, "Why is our family so different from everybody else? All I hear is, Grandpa said this and Daddy said that. It's not *my* fault."

And some years later, Sarah Jane complained, "It embarrasses me when you talk about me on the air."

I don't recall that this bothered me when I was a child. I felt I was a little unique when my peers at the seesaw announced they'd heard me on the air. Dad's show even had a subliminal effect. There was a Parents' Day when we in the third grade were asked to spell new words we'd learned. The bright kids showed off with *electric* and *hydroplane*. I came up with *Musterole*, one of Dad's chest-rub commercials.

But that was thirty years ago, and radio was still a new kind of magic. It must be hard for children today to feel excited about radio when they can not only hear but *see* men on the moon 238,862 miles away. So I respect my children's privacy. And my wife's.

We turn down many invitations. We don't go to theater openings or art-gallery parties or political dinners. What socializing we do, we do with close friends, mostly on weekends.

BILL BREMER: I can understand why John doesn't go out on the town very often. His name makes waves. A couple years ago, my wife and I joined him and Sally for dinner and a movie. Then John suggested, "Why don't we stroll over to the Persian Room and hear Jane Morgan?"

Since we didn't have a reservation, we got only an adequate table from the captain. A few minutes later, the *maître d'* hurried over and told us there'd been some mistake. He moved another party from a table at ringside and seated us there. Obviously, the captain hadn't recognized his name, but the *maître d'* sure did.

What happened after the show started made the whole incident even funnier. Someone had obviously told Jane Morgan that John was there, and since he was playing her records at that time, she sang a couple of songs at our table. Miss Morgan had never met John personally; given a fifty-fifty chance of picking the right guy to sing to—she picked me. It was nice.

SCHUYLER VAN INGEN: Sometimes John's name doesn't help at all. My wife and I once spent several days with the Gamblings in Palm Beach. John reserved a table for dinner at the rather posh Poinciana Playhouse; when we arrived, he told the captain, "You have a reservation for Gambling." The captain looked blank, as only restaurant captains can: "You'll have to go to Puerto Rico for gambling."

SALLY: Anyhow, John's topsy-turvy hours have a lot of advantages. I usually get up by 7:30. Whatever our mood, we don't have to face each other at that dangerous coming-alive time in the morning. And it's so nice to have a man around the house for lunch. I fit my schedule around that and dinner at 6:30. Errands and shopping in the morning; tennis or golf in the afternoon, when he's napping. Often he'll come home right after the show, around noon, and we'll have a lovely afternoon of golf together. I go to bed early, too, at 9:30. It's all nice and cozy until John decides to *plan* something.

I'm gregarious. I look on a meal not as a culinary event but as a social occasion. We enjoy going out with two or three couples for dinner or inviting friends to our home. Beyond that, I enjoy the sheer pleasure of *planning* the get-together—outings, vacations, parties. Sally suspects that in my next incarnation I will come back as a cruise director. I love to see people having a good time, and if I can be the instigator of the good times, I have more fun, too.

For the past ten or eleven Memorial Days we have invited our oldest and closest friends to a family picnic in our backyard. We have three acres and a swimming pool. People start to wander in about noon, after the Main Street parade breaks up. They bring their children and a picnic basket; we supply soda for the youngsters and a keg of beer for the others.

SALLY: It all started with a few close friends, when we first moved to Plandome, and then it escalated. Last year we counted seventy-five or eighty, young and old. John gets the joy of planning, and I get the work. But at the end of the day it's all worthwhile.

The high point is the softball game, sometimes a doubleheader. We don't have many rules—often there are twenty on a side— and we play until we're exhausted. Everybody seems to have fun—kids, parents, dogs—in a genuine togetherness that, I'm afraid, many families don't have anymore. It has an extra dimension of satisfaction for me and Sally, because we've watched those children grow up, year by year. The little tykes who were barely able to swing a bat are now college students trying to hit the ball into Manhasset Bay.

We have an open house on Christmas Eve, too. People come over, with their children, for a couple of hours, to enjoy a buffet and the warmth of meeting and greeting old friends. They come year after year; as some move away, others we have come to know will appear. My parents and Sally's make the event, if they're in this part of the country. Again, there's a feeling of continuity: For some of the young people this is the only chance they have to meet all year.

At the 1971 Christmas party we proudly announced the engagement of Ann to Chris Janelli, a fine young man who's Ann's fellow student at Lake Forest College in Illinois. They were married this past August, and we had the reception at home, under a big tent near the spot of the summer softball game. Chris intends to go on to law school after they both complete their studies at Lake Forest.

Our big adults-only reunion and hullabaloo is the Dartmouth-Princeton football game, every other year at Princeton. During the last ten years I've arranged for a bus to pick up thirty or forty people at our house at about 9 A.M. Everyone brings a picnic lunch and other appropriate refreshments, and we park at a pleasant spot in Princeton for lunch before the game. I'm almost the only Dartmouth man in the group. There are some Princeton graduates, but it's not primarily an old-school outing. After the game, the bus rolls back to our house for supper. And drinks afterward, if there are some who still need them.

In the golf season, a bunch of us organize a Crazy Golf Day. Ten or twelve couples get together for some tricky slices in the rules of the ancient and honorable game. On one hole, you drive with a putter and putt with a driver. On another, you use a pool cue instead of a putter. And play one hole left-handed. Winners receive strange prizes that have been passed back and forth over the years: a wooden leg, or two little battery-powered bears that drink vodka, or the statue of a pretty girl who is obviously pregnant. She's first prize. The winning couples have to give the dinner party the following year.

*

We have lived in our present house for more than ten years. With three children, two dogs, and a couple of cars, our recently added daughter- and son-in-law, we are, I guess, a pretty typical family. I must admit that our house looks bigger now than it did when we bought it. Since John and Ann are both married and living away from home, there are just the four of us now. Sally, Sarah Jane, me, and Frances. A book about the Gamblings wouldn't be complete without mention of Frances De Witt.

Some people would call her our "live-in maid." The more popular words today are "domestic" or "housekeeper." Fran is the wonderful, cheerful, helpful, good friend who lives in our house and helps to keep it a happy home.

*

SALLY: After our sardine-squeeze at Dartmouth, we wanted a place all to ourselves. No apartments, either. But our future was a little hazy when we came to New York—John was still looking for a job—so we rented a small house in Levittown.

That first house had been built in a hurry, on what had been a Long Island potato farm, and we had to put down a $200 security deposit. After a week, we felt we had to do something to jazz up the 10 by 10 living room, which, like the rest of the interior, had been sprayed a blah beige. The lease specified that the tenant couldn't paint inside with a color that would require more than one coat to cover over again. But forest green was the "in" thing that year; we had to have it. Well, the walls were sheetrock, and they must have sopped up ten gallons of paint. I'm surprised the green didn't seep through to the outside. We lost the $200 deposit and I vowed that was the end of my do-it-yourself projects.

SALLY: When Ann arrived in 1952, we needed more room, so we bought a house in Port Washington, L.I. Two years later we moved on to a bigger one, a colonial in Munsey Park in Manhasset. We had a great time furnishing that house with Early American pieces. We'd pile into our car and go antiquing around New Hampshire, Vermont, Pennsylvania. The decor was so early Early American—practically Plymouth Rock—that John began to feel he should wear a three-cornered hat.

We found a beautiful little cherry tilt-top table propping up a door in a Vermont barn. I scraped it and varnished it and rubbed it lovingly. But the varnish never dried; the cocktail glasses stuck to the table. Some of our guests thought they were really bombed when they lifted a martini—and the table came with it. That was the last of my projects.

NICK STEVENSON: I was a neighbor of John's in Munsey Park. There's a story about him still circulating; I don't know if it's apocryphal but I wouldn't put it above him.

Some months after they moved from Munsey Park to Plandome, John and Sally came back to a party and were introduced to a Mrs. Hoar, who'd just moved into the neighborhood. John remarked, "Gee, it's too bad we moved, because it certainly would have been great to have the Gambling house near the Hoar house!"

It was a very friendly street.

SALLY: Our children grew and expanded to fit all the new available space. Early in 1960, John gave me an assignment (he hates to shop): Find a house with four bedrooms. And a fireplace in the master bedroom. So he could enjoy its cheery warmth. But who was going to make that fire at 3 A.M.? Well, I scouted around for months. He wouldn't even set foot in a house if it didn't have that damn fireplace. Then he took one look at this big house in Plandome and told the agent, "We'll take it." No bedroom fireplace, of course, but the house had a dock and overlooked Manhasset Bay, and John was thinking of boats. I was not overjoyed—I knew it would take years to remodel and decorate it properly. But buy it we did.

The boat has been and gone, and we're still here. We love our home, a very happy place for all of us.

I leave most of the interior decorating to Sally. She enjoys it, and she's good at it. Although I like working in the garden, there is just too much to be done in the time I have available, so we have a gardener during the summer. However, I do fuss around with a tomato patch, and I try to keep my hand in at odd but necessary jobs around the house.

> SALLY: Like several months ago, I noticed our freezer was frosting up more than it should. John diagnosed the problem as "leaking air around the door—needs a new gasket." He called a supply house, gave the model number, and they sent a new strip of rubber. For $26. John unscrewed the strip around the edge of the door, and all the insides came out. All over the floor. John tried to put it all together again, but he couldn't close the door. The gasket was too big. He called in a professional repairman, who muttered, "Oh, my God!" and took it all apart again. After he'd put it together—some hours later—he announced, "The gasket is too big." At this point, I felt we might as well do a proper job in the kitchen, so we had a wall ripped out for a new freezer-refrigerator, and more cabinets . . . and a closet.

My little repair job ended up costing over $1,000. But, after all, it was absolutely my last do-it-yourself project.

Our house has received good (but rather exaggerated) reviews in two newspapers. The *Wall Street Journal* called it a "$100,000 Georgian brick home" and *Newsday* labeled it a "twenty-room Georgian mansion." To us, it's just home. Downstairs is pleasantly spacious, with plenty of room for Sally's house plants. We have five bedrooms, plus the two-room office suite on the third floor. The architecture is Long Island Georgian; the decor is bright and sunny.

Outside, it's mostly lawn, shrubs, and some flowers. The swimming pool was added a few years ago and it has become our summertime center for entertaining and relaxing. And even though the boat is gone from the dock, the "crystal-clear waters of Manhasset Bay" are still there.

The house is in our name but the actual owners are the two dogs. It's hard to believe that getting a Newfoundland into this house was a struggle. I've always wanted a Newf. They strike a responsive chord deep inside: they're gentle and intelligent, and anyhow I always liked big dogs.

While I was in school, during World War II, we had a cocker spaniel, Porgy. He bit the butcher right in the middle of . . . rationing. And not only that. My mother had saved ration coupons for months, to buy a roast beef for an anniversary party. It was a four-rib production, which she left to cool in the kitchen. When my father went to carve the meat—disaster! Porgy was rassling the roast under the table. Dad grabbed my baseball bat and bluffed the dog out of the meat. We ate it with appropriate relish, despite what seemed to be teeth marks around the edge. After all, there was a war on. . . . Porgy left us shortly after.

He was followed by a nervous poodle named Demitasse, who lived with us in Munsey Park and, for a while, in Plandome. Demitasse had one great claim to fame. He would eat almost anything, often with digestive difficulties as an aftermath. We never knew why he decided to try the children's crayons; for the next couple of days there were interestingly shaped and brightly colored marks all over our front walk.

As the years passed, I kept talking about "my Newfoundland." I even mentioned it on the air a couple times. A listener, who operated a kennel of Newfs, sent me a book she had written about the breed. Still, Sally felt a Newfoundland was just too enormous a problem, no matter how big the house. I bided my time.

Then one night about four years ago, a strange thing happened. We were going out to dinner and for the first time in our marriage, I was dressed early and waiting for Sally. She had to realign her hem, and she couldn't find the right-shade belt to match her shoes, and all that. I was irritated—we had friends waiting for dinner. Then, young John's car came whizzing up the drive. A Newf puppy was sleeping on the front seat. John had been stuck in traffic, driving back from the kennel in Connecticut. Which explained Sally's stalling.

The family always claims I am never surprised by presents, but that night I was flabbergasted and delighted. We named her Little Bear's Nana. Little Bear after the kennel and the fine heritage from which she came, and Nana after the Newfoundland in the play *Peter Pan*. If you remember, it was Nana who took care of the two children, John and Wendy, on the night Peter Pan spirited them away to Never Never Land.

Nana is a marvelous dog. She's not a lap dog, exactly, at about 135 pounds. But she's big and lovable, gentle and placid. Thank God. What would you do with an excitable dog that big?

Now complications set in. Sarah Jane had always wanted a cat, so we acquired a kitten at a fund-raising auction of the Buckley County Day School, which she attends. (It wasn't difficult—I was the auctioneer.) We named her Taffy, because of her color. And now Nana became a problem: She turned into an old-style dog in the manger. Stuffy and possessive.

Three weeks later, Ann came home from college hugging a small dog, of unknown lineage, with shaggy blonde hair and a coquettish disposition. Ann had christened her Hookah (that's a Far East tobacco pipe), but why, this witness cannot swear to. The dog promptly decided to drop out of college and find a pad at our house.

Well, two newcomers were just too much for Nana, who'd been sole mistress of the house for three years. She sulked and occasionally tried to swallow one of the intruders. So we regretfully agreed to let a neighbor have Taffy. On condition that nine cases of cat-food, which a sponsor had given us to sample, went along with her. A sort of dowry.

Nana and Hookah have established a rough-and-ready *modus vivendi*, despite the preposterous difference in size. Hookah will bite at Nana's ear, chew her tail, do everything but stone this Goliath with a slingshot. All of which Nana tolerates with great goodwill—up to a point. At some imprecise moment, a big, black paw swoops down over Hookah, and she tumbles back, head over tail.

As members of the family, Nana and Hookah are fair game

for conversation on *Rambling With Gambling*. Peter and Jo
Roberts are great animal fanciers (they have two pug dogs and
three drop-in cats) and we'll often discuss our pets' idiosyncrasies on the air.

*

One of my idiosyncrasies is a concern for time—and budget-
ing it. Because so much of my life is governed by the clock
and the calendar. How often we all say, "If I only had enough
time." Time is literally like money. By working hard, you earn
leisure time for the other things which you feel are important.
But then, you've got to budget that time very carefully, just
like money. Otherwise your entire day is devalued, and you
wonder where it's all gone. And was it worth it? I feel that
my community work, for example, is time well spent.

For most of my adult life I've been involved in helping
schools, my church, and the community. When Ann and John
were younger, Sally and I taught Sunday school at the Con-
gregational Church of Manhasset. Sally originally got me involved in volunteer community work. She'd been very active
in the Junior League for a number of years; through that organization she was drawn into a number of community activities,
including most recently the Family Service Association. She
is a member of their Board and heads a committee that plans
and reviews their programs. She is also on the Board of
Directors of the United Fund in Manhasset, and other organizations.

I served as a member of the Board of Directors of the Health
and Welfare Council of Nassau County for seven years, and
as president of the Board for two years. This independent
citizens' group coordinates and plans the health and welfare
work of the county, through both public and private agencies.

For the past five years I have been deeply involved in the
affairs of the Buckley County Day School, in North Hills near
Manhasset. It's an independent school, with about 350 children
in kindergarten through ninth grade, and a forward-looking
program. I've served as trustee for six years and president of

the Board for the last two. Ann and John studied there before Sarah Jane.

Ann later went on to the Emma Willard School, in Troy, N.Y., a girls' boarding school of long tradition and important new ideas. John spent three years at the Hill School, Pottstown, Pa., and then came home to finish his junior and senior high years at Friends Academy here on Long Island. Boarding was not his school bag. Sarah will stay at Buckley through ninth grade and after that . . . well, we'll just have to wait and see.

In all my activities outside the home, Rule One is: no engagements on weekends. That's the only evening prime-time I have. And so most of my community time is expended in meetings during the day or early evenings. The truth is, the amount of help I give to these organizations is more than balanced by the help I get from them. Meeting and talking to people in all walks of life keeps me in touch with the world outside the radio studio. That's the real world.

Sally accuses me of working hard and playing harder, and maybe she's right. I can't help it. One of the things I live for is sports—sailing, skiing, tennis, you name it. But we're all in it together: It's a family affair.

CHAPTER FOURTEEN

THE FAMILY THAT SKIS TOGETHER CONVALESCES TOGETHER

> I often hear you mention your
> wife Sally on the radio. Could
> this be the former Sally Lop-
> packer of Bloomfield, N.J.? I
> played football for Bloomfield
> High—Midge Loppacker and I
> were halfbacks (tailbacks today)
> and Ray Loppacker was right
> end.
>
> C. W. Maguire
> Springfield, N.J.

Right. The sports blood runs thick in our families.

I've always loved boats, big ones or small ones, for racing or just plain sailing. I've had my feet clutching the deck of a sailboat or powerboat ever since I was nine. I still have affectionate memories of my father's second cabin cruiser, a 40-footer called the *John B. II*. She was built late in 1939. We had fun in her for two years; after Pearl Harbor he couldn't get gasoline because of wartime priorities, so he turned her over to the Coast Guard. The *John B. II* served as a submarine picket boat out of Port Jefferson, on the north shore of Long Island Sound. After the war, the Coast Guard returned the boat, but she was far gone by that time and my father sold her. I hear she's still floating around Long Island ports.

My family owned smaller power boats after that, and I had sailboats when we summered in Massapequa. After we bought that beautiful dock with the house at Plandome, we invested in a 37-foot Egg Harbor cruiser named, just like our sailboats, the *JAG*. Sally and I enjoyed her, the children enjoyed her, our

friends enjoyed her. We covered a lot of water, from here to
Maine and Canada and even to Shea Stadium (via Manhasset
Bay to the World's Fair marina) for Jets football games.

ANN: I loved sailing on the *JAG*, even though she was
what the sailboat sailors call a "stinkpot." When I was
younger, I spent about three summers racing sailboats
in Manhasset Bay—Blue Jays and Lightnings. But with
the big boat, it's like—you're actually going someplace.
We had fun.

The family sense of humor got a good stretching on those
cruises. Once when we took the *JAG* up to Edgartown, one
of our favorite spots on Martha's Vineyard, we went ashore
for dinner at a rather fancy restaurant overlooking the harbor.
As I relaxed, I kicked my loafers off under the table (I like to
eat with my shoes off). After dinner, my feet hunted blindly
under the table for my shoes. Nowhere. And then a bubble
of laughter eddied around the restaurant—as Ann retrieved
my shoes at the other end of the room. She and Sally had
secretly kicked them away; then total strangers at other tables
got into the act and propelled the shoes close to the exit door.

JOHN R.: I don't know why, but boats and my grandfather seem to get into the wildest situations. When Ann
and I visited Grandma and Grandpa Gambling in Florida
years ago, he bought an Elgin outboard and boat from
Sears, Roebuck. He bought it partly for us, but I knew he
really wanted one for himself and this was a good excuse.
He had just about everything for that little boat. Seat
cushions, a boat hook, a horn, and compass. I guess he'd
ordered the works down at Sears.
We had a great time that first day, scooting all around
Lake Worth, right near their house. Later, we tied the
boat up carefully at the Sailfish Club, and went back to
Grandpa's house for dinner. About halfway through the
meal, the phone rang. It was the dockmaster at the club.
The boat had sunk . . . right there at the dock . . . right
down to the bottom. Boat, motor, seat cushions, boat
hook, everything. The drain plug must have come loose—
or maybe we'd forgotten all about it.

Grandpa sold the whole thing the next day. Under water.

Another time, Grandpa gave a party on the beach of his house in Old Field. A big clambake for his friends and the people who worked with him at WOR. Must have been 300 guests. Mom, Dad, Ann, and I were on vacation; we sailed out there in a sailboat called *Eventide,* the first cruising boat Dad had ever chartered. And nothing but trouble. After the party, we spent the night sleeping on the boat, anchored in Setauket Harbor. In the morning, I couldn't stand up straight. I wondered how I could have gotten so dizzy on Coke—the boat felt like it was listing at a forty-five-degree angle. It was. During the night, the tide had gone out and we were high and dry. We waded ashore through the mud, up to our waists—it was piggy!—and waited for the tide to float her.

Somebody has said the two happiest days in a sailor's life are the day he buys a boat and the day he sells it. I wasn't ecstatic about selling the *JAG,* but our family interests had changed. We didn't need a boat sitting around all year. Now we charter one for our summer cruises, and we have come full circle to sailboats again.

Our son, John, got us all into skiing about ten years ago. He picked it up on ski trips from school. I had never skied while I was at Dartmouth; I'd been occupied at the radio station while the other guys were out on the slopes.

I'm sure you've heard people say that skiing is a great family sport. Take it from a family, it is. Up until a couple of years ago, when we joined the Windham Mountain Ski Club in the Catskills, we took our skiing pretty much where we found it. We spent two wonderful vacations at Vail, in Colorado, and have had good, fair, and poor weekends at various ski areas in New England. But, of course, that's about par for skiing in our part of the world.

Young John is the strongest skier in the family, despite having broken both of his legs at various times over the past twelve years. Ann is a very smooth skier, and Sarah Jane is probably going to end up the best in the family. Our daughter-in-law, Chris Gambling, and our son-in-law, Chris Janelli, are also ski nuts, so the group grows.

I love to ski. I would have a hard time deciding whether I like skiing or sailing better. In both sports there is a marvelous feeling of freedom, of pitting your own personal skills against nature rather than against another person. Whether it's snow and a steep trail, or wind and water, I enjoy this kind of test.

> BILL BREMER: John is a great competitor. Everything he does, he does at ninety miles an hour. . . . He and Sally are the all-time great teams in whatever they do. She moves in wondrous ways . . . she's 50 percent of the whole operation.

> SALLY: I have to admit I was the last one to fall in line. I'm not afraid of contact sports—I played a rough game of field hockey in school. I just didn't relish sliding straight down a mountain on a couple of boards. It took a while, but now I love it. I'm not daring, because I worry about breaking an arm or a leg. That thought never occurs to the two men and the two girls.

Young John broke a leg during one of the Vail, Colorado, vacations. This one really curled my hair. We had flown out there with six youngsters (everybody had a friend) and came back with seven . . . one joined us after the first week. One of the girls came down with sun poisoning; a boy had strep throat; I had a sunburnt lower lip that became infected. But the skiing was great, and a good time was had by all. The melodramatic finale came Easter Sunday, when we drove back to take the plane for home. We left Vail, on the west side of the Continental Divide, in two cars, with thirty-nine pieces of luggage and John R.'s leg in a cast. Sally and Sarah and her friend were in my lead car; all the teen-agers crammed in with John R., as we twisted and turned up this narrow mountain road. After one turn, I realized there was no car behind. A jeep caught up with us and the driver yelled at me, from under his hair, "Is there a red car following you?"

"Yes and no," I answered, trying to be accurate.

"They had a flat tire. Back thataway."

We found the red car teetering beside a sheer drop at the side of the road. Four of the youngsters were in the front seat, to anchor it; the luggage was strewn all over the road, and John, on crutches, was supervising the tire change. "Don't worry," he called out. "What more can happen?" I didn't want to think of the possibilities.

We got to the Denver airport exactly four minutes before the plane was due to take off. I rushed up to the clerk at the counter. "I've got seven kids and two adults, one is a stand-by and one is flying first-class instead of coach because his leg is busted. I've got thirty-nine pieces of luggage, and two rental cars that have to be returned. What should I do?" With an imperturbability that will always endear that man to me, he said, "Mr. Gambling, just get on the plane. We'll take care of everything."

We did. And he did.

> SALLY: As I was catching my breath, the stewardess bubbled with admiration. "So you're the lady with the nine children?"
>
> For an instant, I panicked. Were there nine? I counted the group and carefully explained, "I only have three myself, but there are a total of seven children. Plus me and our cruise director.
>
> She blinked and rechecked her list: "Then where is this Mr. Gambling?"

In winter we play tennis indoors, in a club at Port Washington. I played some in high school and college, but never well enough to make a team. Sally is good and getting better; I have a hard time beating Ann, and doubles against her and John are an even match. Sarah Jane takes lessons in the summer and will, I think, become a truly formidable player.

Despite all this exercise, I have a real problem keeping my weight down. I gained about fifteen pounds when I stopped smoking several years ago, and I still face those bizarre hungers mentioned in an earlier chapter. The sins of my childhood are coming back to haunt me.

I was always a skinny kid. Mother set out three meals a day, which I dutifully ate. Yet it was never enough. I drifted into picking at any food in sight, just to fill up those gaps in my hunger. Anything. I ate like a plague of locusts. One of my favorite desserts was a mayonnaise sandwich: two slices of white bread with an inch of goo between them. I would think nothing of slipping into the pantry, opening a can of condensed mushroom soup and eating it, cold and condensed. My grandmother Dora *tsk-tsked* worriedly over this: "You'll get worms."

By the time I reached high school, I was a 5-foot-9, 135-pound bundle of wires. The gag around Horace Mann was: Johnnie has to drink chocolate milk so you can't see through him. Not long ago I attended the reunion of our class of '47. Charley Avedesian, our former football coach for whom I'd given my all on the varsity, looked me over and exclaimed, "My God, Gambling! If you'd had the weight then that you have now—we would have been city champs." I don't know . . . if I'd had all these 190 pounds twenty-five years ago, I might not be able to get my face close to a microphone today.

I really have to work to pull my weight down. The simple truth is, I can't shake the pick-and-lick habit. I used to come home and pick, then have lunch. I've given up lunch; now I just come home and pick. Sally makes a great barley soup, which I prefer at 3:30 A.M., cold, when it has the consistency of cabinetmaker's glue.

> SALLY: Our vices complement each other. Mine is—not being able to throw anything away. I come into the kitchen and find a trail of dishes and pots that John's been picking at, all over the counters and table and refrigerator top. He might lose a few more pounds if I could bring myself to throw away a few hors d'oeuvres. Maybe I'll start an organization to fight this compulsive hoarding—Appetizers Anonymous.

Next week I think I'll go on a diet.

Every time we plan a vacation, a friend is sure to murmur, "Gosh—*again?*" The truth is, my WOR contract allows me to take five weeks off each year, and no more than three weeks at one stretch. In this day and age, five weeks away isn't *that* unusual. It seems to stretch on and on because I spread it out through the year. A week here—ten days there. We take a few days off in the spring and fly down to Pinehurst, N.C., with friends for a long weekend of golf. And recently Sally has taken our girls to Nassau or Puerto Rico for their spring school vacation. I usually try to join them for the weekend, and maybe an extra day.

Of course, Christmas, New Year's, the Fourth of July, and the rest of the normal work holidays are just another workday in the radio business, so our vacation time has to be planned accordingly. Sometimes, though, we still are able to do things on the spur of the moment.

> SCHUYLER VAN INGEN: For my fiftieth birthday, my wife and I flew down to Puerto Rico to celebrate. John was very helpful—even carried our bags to the plane. Next morning, the people in the room next door started banging on the wall—it was John and Sally.

During the past few winters we have rented a little farmhouse perched on a hillside in Hensonville, N.Y. This tiny, friendly village bills itself as "the gem of the Catskills," and is only minutes from the Windham Mountain Ski Club. It has become our regular weekend hideway when the snow is on the ground. Happily, it's less than a three-hour drive from Long Island.

Occasionally, though, Sally and I like to get far away, without the youngsters. For three consecutive winters, we have cruised with other couples in the Grenadines. These are the lovely isolated Leeward Islands, well south of Puerto Rico and the Virgin Islands, where the outside world virtually ceases to exist. Recently, with three other couples on two chartered sailboats, we cruised from island to island for two weeks. We didn't see a newspaper, we didn't hear a single radio news broadcast. I think this sort of total get-away-from-it-all is very important. Batteries must be recharged, viewpoints refreshed, heads cleared, and values realigned.

It was interesting to find, when we returned to New York, that virtually nothing of real importance had happened while we were away.

*

I've always had an itch to fly a plane. It may date back to those formative years when I was building model biplanes that never got off the ground. About six years ago, I began taking flying lessons at Flushing Airport, a cramped patch of ground near LaGuardia in Queens. Don Foley, an ex-fighter pilot, was my instructor. And I had my quota of mortifying minutes while I accumulated eighty hours in the air.

The most frightening thing about your first solo flight is, you never know when it's coming. It usually happens after fifteen or twenty hours of instruction, provided you and your instructor have survived a couple dozen takeoffs and landings. I thought I was doing rather well one day when Don Foley muttered darkly, "I'm not going to fly with you anymore. I'm likely to get killed." He climbed out of the plane, then smiled. "Okay, take it up."

Well, any idiot can get a plane off the ground and any fool can keep a plane in the air. What separates the pilots from the walking wounded is the landing. I'd always heard that when you are really scared, your knees literally knock together. Up until that day at Flushing, it had never happened to me.

No problem on takeoff. A couple of smooth turns around the airport and out over the Throgs Neck Bridge—wow! I'm a pilot, and this whole flipping airplane is mine to fly. . . . It is a real thrill, believe me. But then you also have to get the thing back down on the ground.

I made a passable approach, my speed and altitude were fine as I came in over the end of the runway, and I flared out just as I had been taught. The wheels touched, I cut power, hit the brakes not too hard, and I was down.

But don't ever let anyone tell you knees don't knock.

Don congratulated me. "Now do a couple more landings, just for practice!" I did. Not as well as the first one, but with some dash, I thought.

Don then proposed we drop over to the Terrace Restaurant at LaGuardia for a drink and lunch to celebrate my airworthiness. I ordered a double martini, to match Don's. After all the previous tension, my blood vessels must have expanded to the diameter of water mains . . . the alcohol flowed straight to my brain. Suddenly, I was flying again, in a tropical storm, without wings, without an airplane. I made some lame excuse about work to avoid lunch, floated out to my car, and set my course for home. I must have navigated by automatic pilot. That drive home was more death-defying than anything I'd faced up in the air.

For sheer sleep-defying suspense, let me tell you about my "emergency landing" with Fred Feldman. Fred, who used to be a jet-pilot instructor for the Air Force, volunteered to sit beside me as I flew down to Pottstown, Pa., to pick up John R. I needed some flying time before I tried for my license, and this was a practical way to get it. Sarah Jane, who was about seven, went along for the ride, in the back seat of the single-engine Piper Cherokee.

Fred tested me with several flying problems on the way. One was an emergency-landing procedure. He cuts the throttle and what do I do? That's easy. We're up about 3,000 feet. I find a cleared farm field, glide down, go into my landing approach, then lower my flaps as if I'm going to land. Don Foley usually waited until I reached 800 feet; he'd grade me good or bad, and then I'd hit the throttle and up we'd go again. Well, here I am in my glide, the engine barely turning over—and Fred just sits there.

We drift down to 500 feet, 400 . . . I can feel Sarah Jane breathing hard on my neck, and that cornfield is zooming up in front of me. What the devil is Fred waiting for? But I don't want to chicken out. When that corn begins to look as high as an elephant's eye, I mutter to Fred, "Do you really expect me to land there?"

"For godssake!" he cries, "get out of here! I've been waiting for *you* to make a move!"

I never got my license. By the time I had passed all the requirements for the examination, I realized I didn't really have enough free time to stay proficient. Flying a plane is not the kind of thing you do casually, at odd moments. I was rather wistful and at loose ends after I made the decision to give it up. I have an idea, though, that WOR management exhaled a collective sigh of relief. So did Sally.

John R. earned his private pilot's license as a senior-year project in high school. He hasn't done much flying since he's been married, but we both talk about getting into it again. Like skiing and sailing, we see it as another match of our skills against the elements.

Sarah Jane told me the almost-landing in the cornfield was real fun. She wants to learn to fly just as soon as she is old enough.

CHAPTER FIFTEEN

DOING YOUR OWN THING

> My wife and I are regular morn-
> ing listeners . . . I remember
> well, back in the 1920s, when I
> woke up to the one, two, three,
> four of John B. Gambling. And
> I hope I will be around to hear
> the third generation, when your
> son starts his program. He better
> not let us down.
>
> Roland H. Babb
> New York City

The future? I'm all for it. I'm only forty-two, and my present contract runs through December 31, 1974. I hope I still have a lot of years at WOR.

I intend to grow and bend with the winds of change. They're coming, of course, in radio and all broadcasting. What was the Pepsi Generation is now growing into the Budweiser Genera-tion. The World War II babies have grown up. And they are exploding the often-quoted myth "Soon, half the population of the United States will be under twenty-five." Almost every-body believed this bit of fantasy; it seems to have been popu-larized in a speech some years ago by Lyndon B. Johnson. It is just not true. People are living longer, and the birth rate is declining sharply.

The New York Times said on April 3, 1967: "According to the Census Bureau, only 40 percent of the population is now under twenty-one. The Bureau figures also indicate that there is no time in the near future when the majority of the popula-tion will be under twenty-five. . . ." In fact, a recent bulletin (February 23, 1972) of the U.S. Bureau of Labor Statistics reported that between 1950 and 1970 the number of persons aged forty-five and over grew at a faster rate than the total U.S. population—44 percent as opposed to 34 percent. I like young people, they are the future; but let us not lose our heads. The population is growing older, not younger.

Since the appeal of *Rambling With Gambling* is mainly to people over twenty-five, I don't foresee any important changes in our format. As Dad used to say, "You don't rewrite a hit." The New York area has seen great dislocations in the ethnic population; radio stations have been orienting toward the interests of blacks, Puerto Ricans, all the minority groups, and all age groups. Our audience has been 90 percent white. I hope that this will change.

I expect eventually, to make some personal changes, too. I welcome the daily challenge of the show, but the hours are long and demanding. I look forward, sometime, to doing less than the thirty hours a week I now work. I've always hankered to own my own radio station. I'd like to be in the cool position of not broadcasting. Someday I'd like to wear shorts to work and take long vacations.

I guess I'm fantasizing about the easy life in the sunny South or Far West—a station already in operation, an established one needing improvement that can use my experience. It may be losing money in a market that's crying out for a good-music station or for rock or, possibly, for a format like our show. Mostly it will require the courage to change. And that is only done after you've gone through more soul search than research.

I've discussed buying a station with our son, just as my father did with me. I turned management down to work in New York; I don't know what John will do.

Will John succeed me in *Rambling With Gambling?* It's up to him, if he wants to try and, of course, if he has the ability. So far, his pattern of enthusiasm for radio is almost a mirror image of mine, twenty years ago.

JOHN R.: When I was seventeen, I got a summer job, working as a production assistant for Dad. I came in at 7 A.M. and helped Bill McEvilly to contact the helicopter and monitor CBS's helicopter news. I filed records and

things like that. Also I worked on putting together the
tape material for the Saturday show.

Next summer, I worked for WOR as a program super-
visor. It was a full eight-hour-a-day job, 9 P.M. to 5 A.M.
and sometimes 9 A.M. to 5 P.M. It was a basic course in
production for me: Getting together the cartridges for all
the shows; making sure the commercials were in the
right studio for the right show; having cartridges made
for the commercials. And logging commercials. When
a commercial is aired, the time and duration have to be
entered on a log, to comply with FCC regulations.

Of course, I am always hearing, "Are you going to do
your father's show when he retires?" That just rolled
off my back at first. I never paid much attention to it.

But the more I get into radio at Boston U., the more
I enjoy it. In October 1970, when I was a sophomore, I
took a chance and applied to WTBU. A week later, I got
the call. WTBU is a carrier-current station, not over-the-
air. It transmits through the school's own power lines, so
it can be heard only on campus, in the dorms. It's not a
big operation.

I went on from 7 to 9 in the morning, with music,
news, weather, and a lot of time checks. I worked five
days a week, and that's a lot of program for that kind of
station. Most of the guys worked one day.

I really enjoyed it. Even getting up at 6 in the morning. It gets very cold in Boston at 6 A.M. In fact, it's
freezing. I often have to do the show in my big, heavy,
insulated flight jacket. [Nothing can be as cold as
6 A.M. in Lebanon, N.H., in a house trailer—Dad.] I
turn on the equipment and at 7 I go on. It's a very
lonely feeling, to sit by yourself in front of a microphone
and talk. I know, in the back of my mind, that somebody
is listening out there. But getting through that "alone"
feeling is probably one of the most difficult things I've
had to learn about the business of broadcasting.

This year, I am continuing my show and also have
become station manager, for which I receive a stipend
of $125 a month. That helps a married guy who doesn't
want to be too much of a burden on parents. [That's
$125 more than I made as station manager at WDBS—
Dad.]

I'm not sure if I'll be in the broadcasting end or the

business end, but I do want to be in radio. When TV came in, in the fifties, a lot of smart people thought radio would be wiped out. Well, radio is bigger and better than it ever was. Much more varied programming, and much better quality reception because of FM.

Eventually AM radio will have to program just news, talk, and weather, and leave the music to FM. The FM good-music format is getting old now. It'll have to change soon. But radio always changes. If you stand still in radio, you go right down the pipe. I think radio has barely scratched its future potential.

I completely agree with John's estimate of radio's future. There is excitement ahead. And if I were to consult a clouded crystal ball, my hunch would be that John's decision will be the same as mine was two decades ago. Give New York a try— if New York will have you. Nothing would make a father prouder.

*

To establish any sort of personal philosophy, you have to decide what is important in your life. For the last twenty-three of my forty-two years, the most vital anchor for me has been my family. I've been fortunate to have a profession that I find challenging and satisfying—most of the time. Still, my primary concern has been to create enough time, within the demands of my work, to make my family the center of my life.

As a result, the six of us—Sally, the three children, our daughter-in-law—have been able to do so much together. Our new son-in-law makes us seven. I don't for a moment believe that togetherness is a panacea for all family problems—we've had our divisions and dissensions, as any family must. But the closeness we've developed over the years has turned many a mountain into a molehill. The essence of our happiness as a family is mutual love and respect among all of us.

I don't believe you can be a "pal" to your children. Differences in age and generation will always create a different view of life. And rightly so, otherwise the world would stand still.

How have Sally and I brought up our children? With mutual respect for the intelligence and integrity of each child and by being quite permissive. Yes, they have had a great deal of freedom. John, Ann, and Sarah Jane have been allowed to do much of what they wanted to do. However, they have also known that when boundaries on their activities *have* been set, they cannot overstep them. Some punishment, some curtailment of their freedom would automatically result. Never any doubt about that. If there is one word to describe a parent's obligation toward children, it is *consistency*. If you say one thing today, don't say the opposite tomorrow. It creates doubts, weakness, and then anger.

I think consistency is the cement in most personal relationships. You can't be an S.O.B. one day and the most lovable guy in the world the next. It just doesn't work. It doesn't make sense. Sure, people change mentally and physically every day —cells are born and die within us every instant of our lives— but these are gradual changes. Man is a reasoning animal; this and wearing clothes are what distinguish him from the animals. If you strive to be consistent in your attitude and actions toward the people you love and the world around you, life becomes so much easier. And the world is so much more pleasant. For them and for you.

I've always tried to be reasonable and consistent in my personal and professional relationships. This may explain why my attitude toward life is so optimistic. I don't know which came first: Am I optimistic because I am reasonable, or reasonable because I am optimistic? No matter. It works.

My political philosophy is liberal, somewhere left of center. I'm basically optimistic about the changes possible in our society. If you could categorize my voting, it has been independent. I've voted for Democrats and I've voted for Republicans, and sometimes, I'm afraid, I've voted for Tweedledum and Tweedledee. I try to vote for the man who will do the best job.

I find myself agreeing more with young people and disagreeing more with old people. But the young must learn to be patient with the old; the old must learn to heed the voice of youth. I've always tried to establish a rapport with the under twenty-fives—our own offspring, their friends, youngsters I meet wherever I go—because these are the people who have the responsibility for making this world a better place to live in. Those of us who are spreading into middle age have already accomplished pretty much all that we're ever going to do. We've made an impact, and we're not going to change ourselves a great deal in the thirty or forty years we may have left. And since we can't change ourselves, we're hardly likely to change the world. So any improvement in the quality of life on this planet will have to be created by those younger than ourselves. That's why I feel it's so important to establish some kind of dialogue with them. You cannot make them think your way; but you can share ideas, and hopefully help them see more clearly what they are capable of accomplishing.

I don't believe, of course, that all young people are automatically bright and noble knights of the future. I wish they could have a little more historical perspective. Somehow, they assume that the windmills they tilt against have never existed before . . . anytime or anywhere in the world. Must society be destroyed before it can be improved? Strangely, today's young people can't seem to relate to any political or social situation that occurred before they were born. When I was fifteen or twenty, it seems to me, we knew more history. The world cannot have become that much more complex in the two decades. If they want to make changes, they really should know how changes were made in the past and, more important, why they succeeded or failed.

This lack of historical perspective may be what psychologists have categorized as the new generations' demand for "instant gratification." No need to plan or work for anything—just yell for it and it's yours. If that's true, it is we—the parents—who've let them drift into some kind of eternal Disneyland. I'm all for seizing the day and living it to the full. In the seventeenth century, Thomas Hobbes described the natural state of man as "solitary, poor, nasty, brutish, and short." Thank God, a lot has changed since then, but life is still very short. It should be as worthwhile and as pleasant as we can make it, for ourselves and those around us. But something has gone before us, and something will follow after. For young people to lock themselves into the world of "special—today only!" is a dangerous blindness.

As I look to the future, one fact about our society is clear to me: Our country's priorities, the things we are willing to spend our money for, are wildly out of kilter. The billions we spend for military hardware, which somehow always exceeds estimated costs and then quickly becomes obsolete . . . the billions we sink into never-ending roads, paving over what's left of a green and fertile land . . . the billions of dollars we shoot into outer space . . . all these things have to be put into clearer perspective.

How can we rationalize these expenditures when we still virtually ignore the below-subsistence poverty of millions of Americans? Consider how many schools just *one* billion dollars will build and staff. Consider, too, that we still do not provide health services very effectively, nor do we do a good job in taking care of the elderly. And we have an utterly wretched and callous record in the care of mental incompetents. There is so much that is good in this country, yet so much more to be done. I think we must all take a long, hard look at how our tax dollars are being spent.

*

You hear and read so much about the "moral revolution" creeping through this country. . . . America's morals are decaying, is the cry. We're sinking into degeneracy. . . . Balderdash! I don't believe morals change very much. I'm not sure that the basic morality of the outwardly stiff and stuffy Victorian era is a great deal different from the moral climate of the 1970s. What is different is our *awareness* of what's going on, every minute of every day.

I firmly believe that 200 or 300 years from now, when historians look back at our century, the revolution they'll recognize will not be men walking on the moon (which is, indeed, a fantastic achievement) or the series of destructive wars this century has been afflicted with. It will be our communications—the Century of Communication. Possibly I'm being too subjective, but the most remarkable change in our world has been the incredible proliferation and penetration of instant communication.

When you think of the isolation of people at the turn of this century, even in the cities, compared to our all-pervasive communication via satellite, TV, radio, telephone, film, and hundreds of new devices now on drawing boards, you realize our planet is a far different place than it was even fifty years ago. "No man is an island" John Donne said. We all become less and less of an island each day. Even when he wants to, man finds it hard to hide, to be by himself, for even a little while.

It is this interaction, this communication, this talking about morality, filming it, showing it, televising it, that has stripped the covers off our self-imposed Puritan-Victorian heritage. Twentieth-century man has not changed. The shell he built up around himself is being peeled away electronically. His true feelings were always there, right from the beginning; but today fewer and fewer people are paying hypocritical lip-service to convention. If our new-found communication creates a more honest, realistic view of our selves and our world, it will be a genuine revolution.

Doing your own thing—that's a great breakthrough. If the younger generation has contributed nothing else, it has shown us that way of life. When you do your own thing, you don't really have to worry about what the neighbors think, or keeping up with the Joneses—all the hypocritical things our generation has rightly been accused of.

These, then, are some of the things I believe in. They have worked for me and for my family because we have faith in our ideals—and ourselves. Sally and I have had a genuinely close relationship. She has not been tightly involved in my professional life, and that's the way we've wanted it. When I come home from work, when I settle down with my family, I want to leave that radio life behind. But all the big decisions, we make together. She has been my single most important support and help through all the difficult times from the very beginning. Her understanding and love have carried me over the conflicts of hours and time and sleep and all the rest of it. A friend has said that Sally is 50 percent of the Gambling combination; I'd make that 150 percent.

We don't always agree, of course. We don't always think the same road will get us to the same destination. But that same determination that overcame a lot of miles and a lot of parental objection, back when we were in school, has seen us through to today. And the love that was kindled at that football game a long time back has simply become deeper. Both John and Ann have married young. Sally and I didn't think they were too young. We just hope that their marriages are as happy, as full, as satisfying as ours has been.